LEFT HANDED
THE CHORD BOOK

By Tom Owen

3   1

×

○

① ② ③

○

**A Simple and Practical Guide
to Chord Identification**

Tinpot publishing

Jacket and layout: Tinpot publishing
Independently published by Tinpot publishing

www.tinpotbooks.com
First edition 2018

ISBN: 9781726630047

Hi

It is estimated that 10% of the world is left handed and a further 1% of those are musicians.

Its amazing to think that players from this tiny percentage have produced talents such as Jimi Hendrix, Tony Iommi, Kurt Cobain, Albert King, Paul McCartney and Ali Campbell to name but a few and that doesn't even take into account left-handed people who play right-handed.

I first encountered problems for the left handed guitarist when a member of my own family wanted to learn to play. Several visits to various music stores soon showed the evident lack of help provided - the most common advice being, "Use a mirror."

This is my attempt in helping to redress that balance.

The Left Handed CHORD Book contains over 500 chords arranged for the left handed player. Presented visually by simple diagrams it is suitable for both novice or professional players alike.

The following few pages will help you set up your guitar and learn to read these diagrams.

I hope you find it useful and I wish you many happy hours of playing.

Tom Owen

CONTENTS

Introduction

You have your guitar and you may now need to re-string it for a left handed player. The strings from the top to the bottom as you hold the instrument are Low E (the thickest string), followed by A, D, G, B and High E (the thinnest string) and are illustrated here at the head of the guitar before it reaches the tuning pegs.

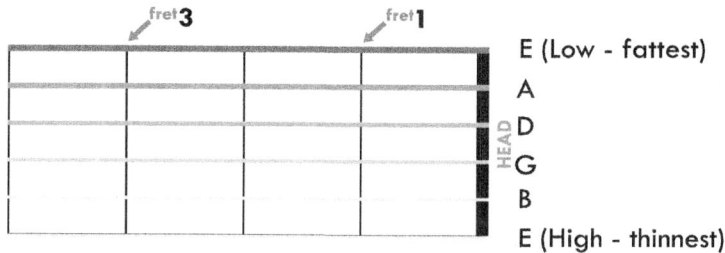

The **numbers on the top (3 & 1)** are the **fret** bars which can be easily located along your guitar neck as dots or inlays which can be seen on the face of the fingerboard. This book also gives some examples of higher chords (above the 12th Fret) which can only be played on specially designed acoustics with a cutaway or on an electric guitar.

Get in Tune, get a TUNER !

This is an essential tool for any musician. Tuning pitches, forks or boxes can be purchased cheaply from any good retail outlet. Alternatively - If your Lower E is roughly in tune you can use the diagram below. The grey ○ means that the string should be played (this is called **OPEN** and will be repeated in the chord boxes).

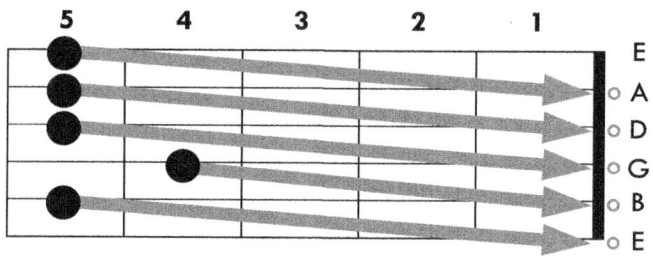

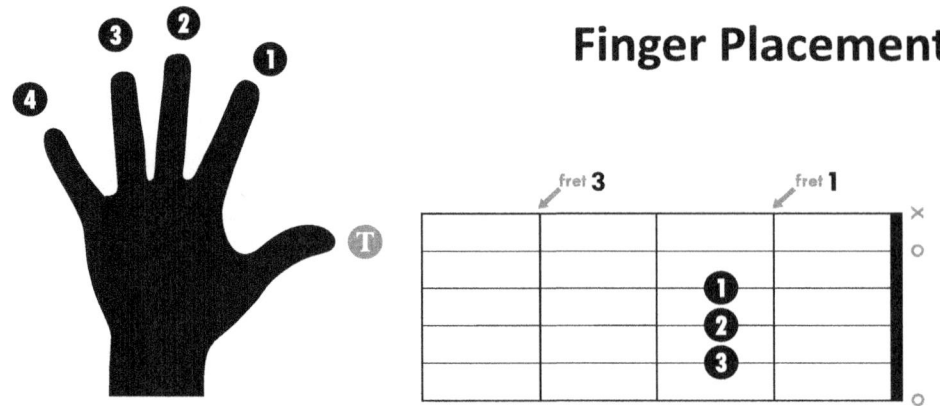

Finger Placement

The corresponding fingers on the silhouette need to be placed in the same position of the marked **fret** number to make a chord. The grey O is played and the grey X is not. You may find it easier to use different finger combinations but if learnt this way it will enable you to move through different chord progressions more comfortably.

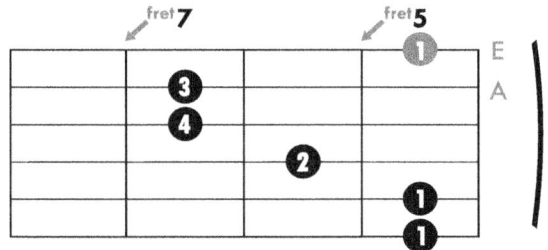

In the illustration above the bowed line indicates that all 6 strings need to be held down with an extended finger (in this case your 1st or index finger. This is called a **barré** and initially will be difficult to do but practice will make it good. Some guitars (especially electric ones) have a thinner neck and some players are more comfortable using their thumb to cover the lower E and

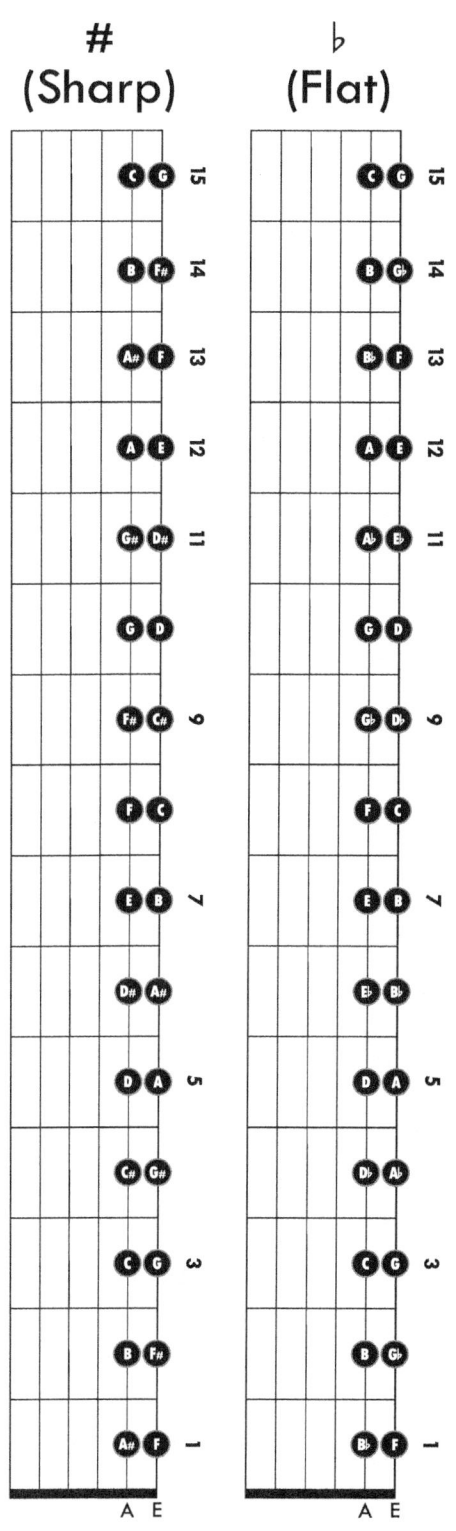

| # (Sharp) | ♭ (Flat) |

Root Notes

MAIN CHORDS

There are only 7 main chords - these are:

A B C D E F G

Inbetween these are **Sharps #** (higher) and **Flats ♭** (lower).

A	A#/B♭	B
C	C#/D♭	D
D	D#/E♭	E
F	F#/G♭	G
G	G#/A♭	A

The **#** and ♭ are the same for each corresponding chord above and below. So if you want to find **C#** it is also the same as **D♭**

From here you can explore the many different combinations open to you. Different examples can be found in the **Terminology** section on the last page of this book.

	PAGE		PAGE		PAGE
F#/Gb	**201**	**G**	**222**	**G#/Ab**	**243**
F#m	202	Gm	223	Abm	244
F#7	203	G7	224	Ab7	245
F#m7	204	Gm7	225	Abm7	246
F#maj7	205	Gmaj7	226	Abmaj7	247
F#5	206	G5	227	Ab5	248
F#6	207	G6	228	Ab6	249
F#m6	208	Gm6	229	Abm6	250
F#9	209	G9	230	Ab9	251
F#m9	210	Gm9	231	Abm9	252
F#maj9	211	Gmaj9	232	Abmaj9	253
F#dim7	212	Gdim7	233	Abdim7	254
F#11	213	G11	234	Ab11	255
F#13	214	G13	235	Ab13	256
F#m13	215	Gm13	236	Abm13	257
F#add9	216	Gadd9	237	Abadd9	258
F#sus4	217	Gsus4	238	Absus4	259
F#7sus4	218	G7sus4	239	Ab7sus4	260
F#6/9	219	G6/9	240	Ab6/9	261
F#aug	220	Gaug	241	Abaug	262
F#7#9	221	G7#9	242	Ab7#9	263

A

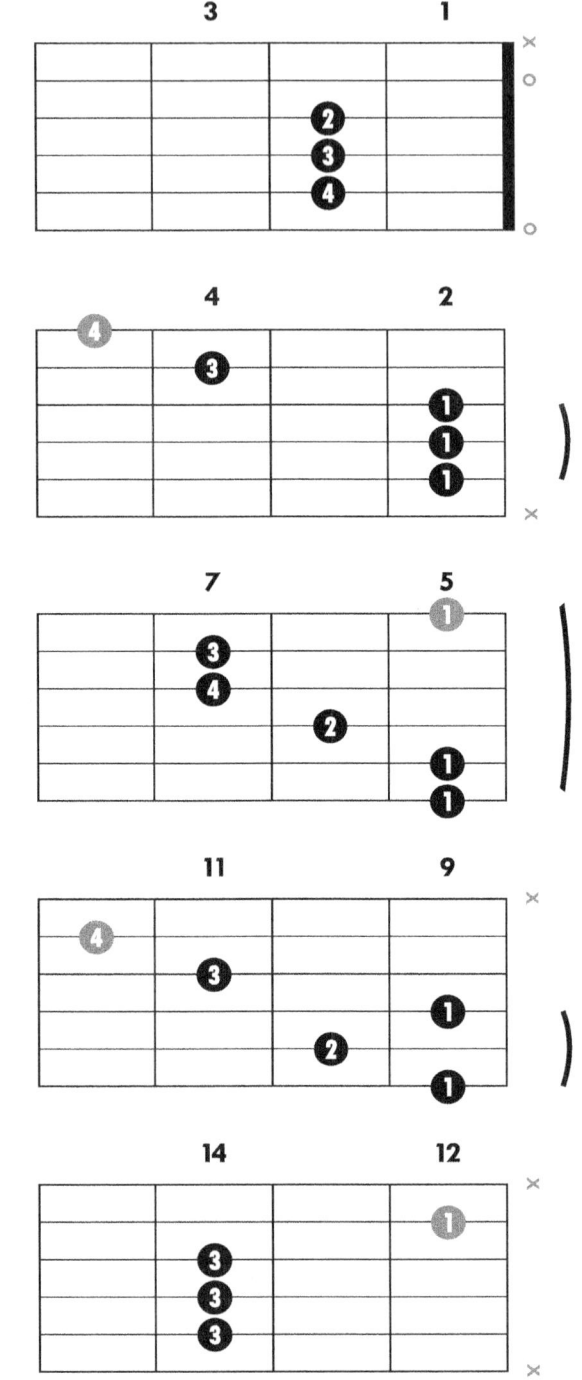

Am

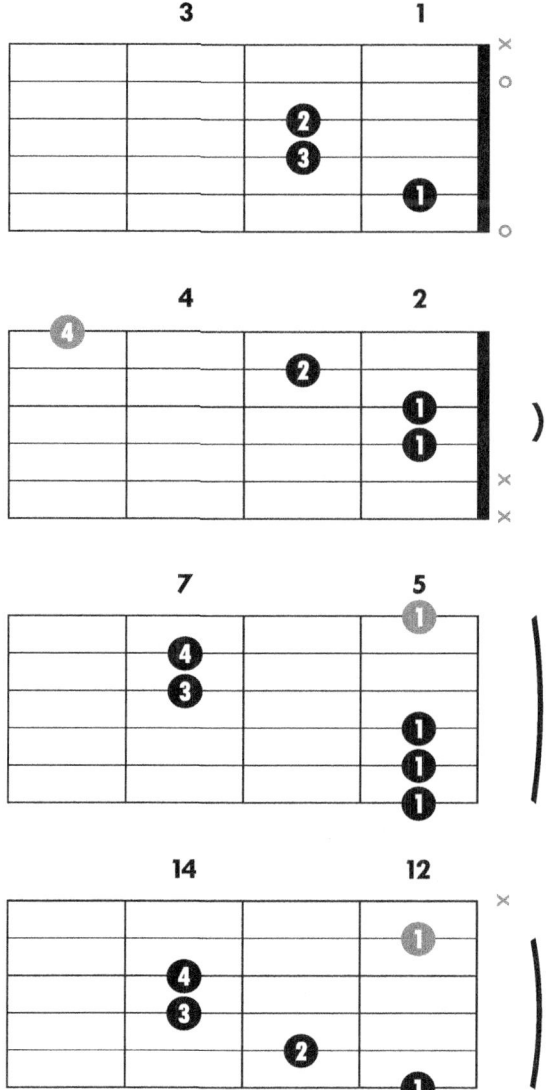

A7

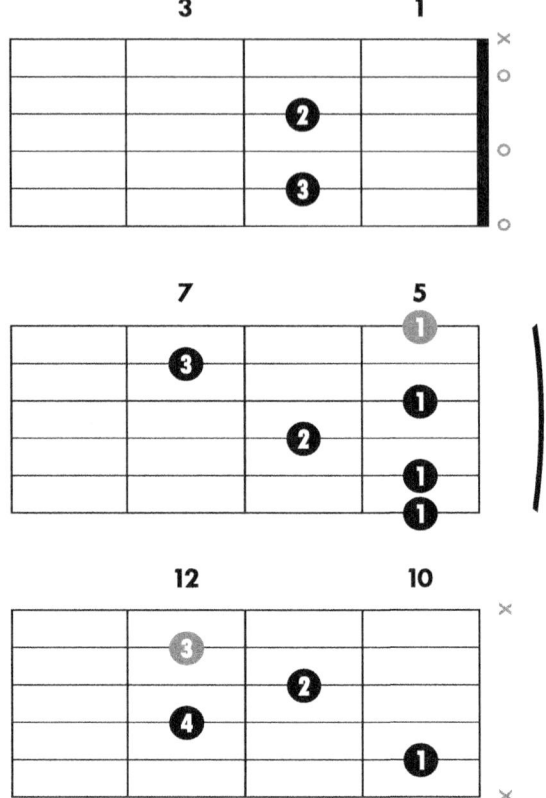

Am7

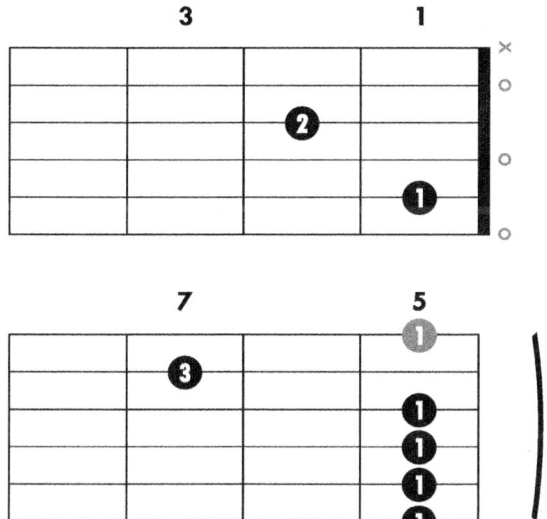

Amaj7

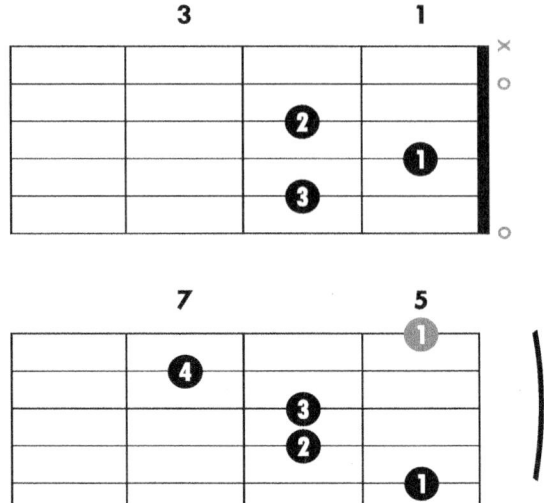

A5

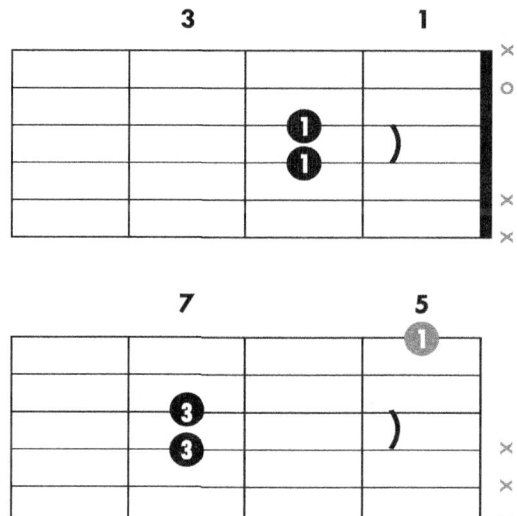

A6

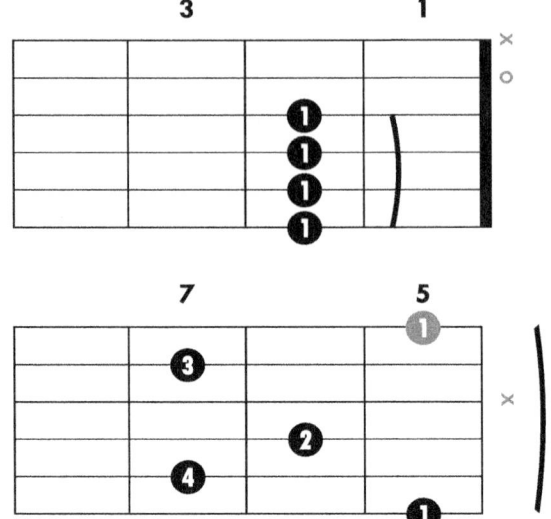

Am6

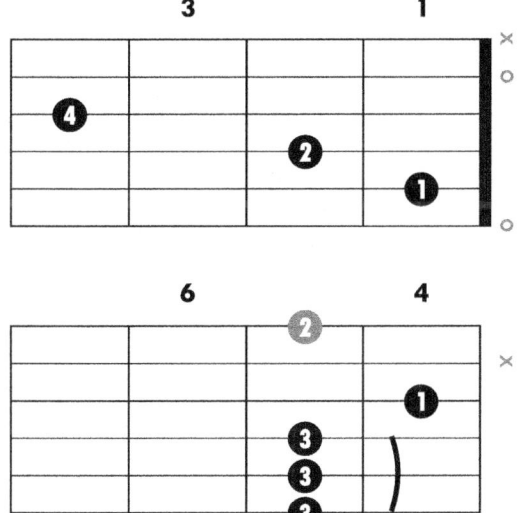

A9

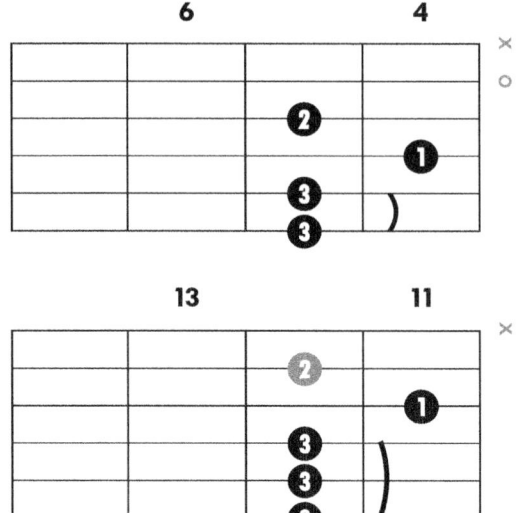

Am9

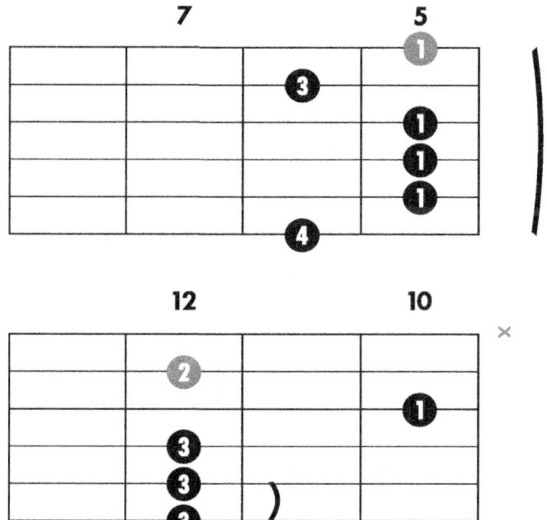

Amaj9

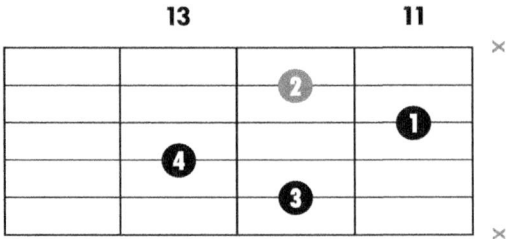

Adim7

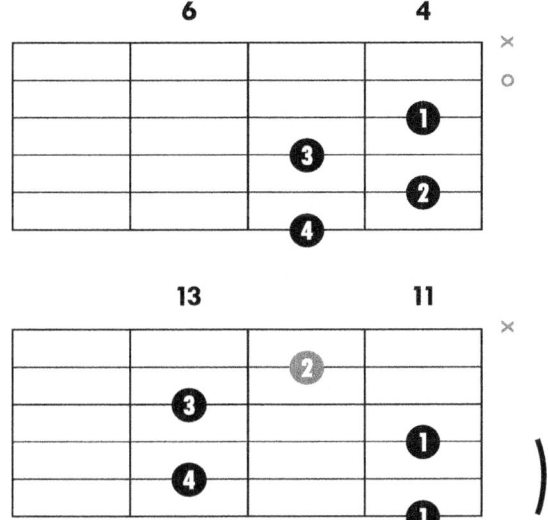

A11

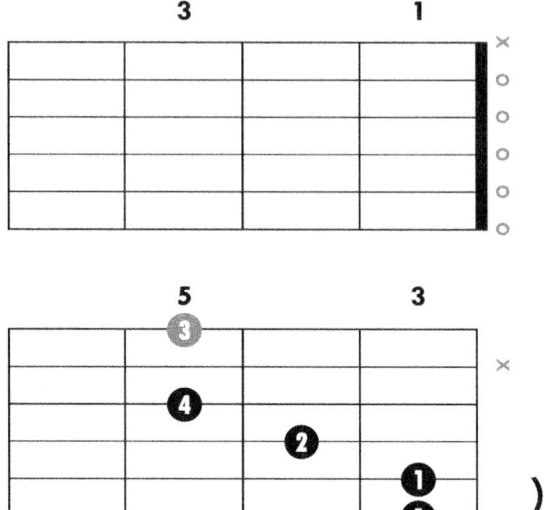

A13

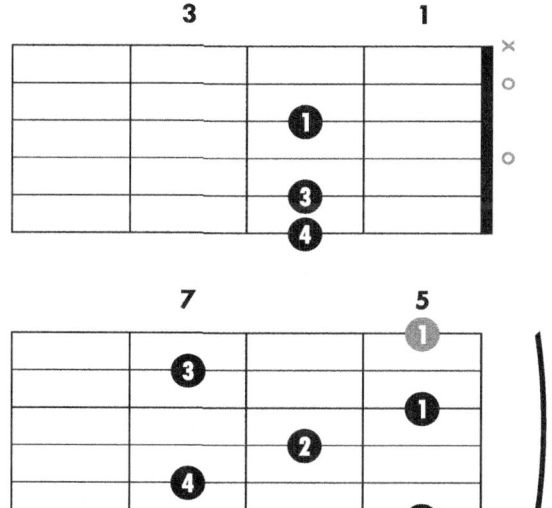

Am13

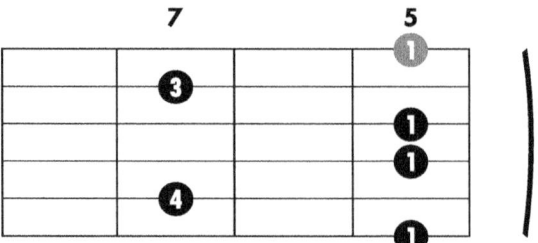

Aadd9

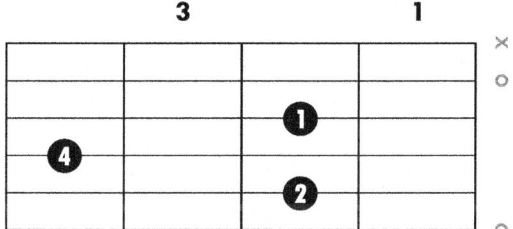

Asus4

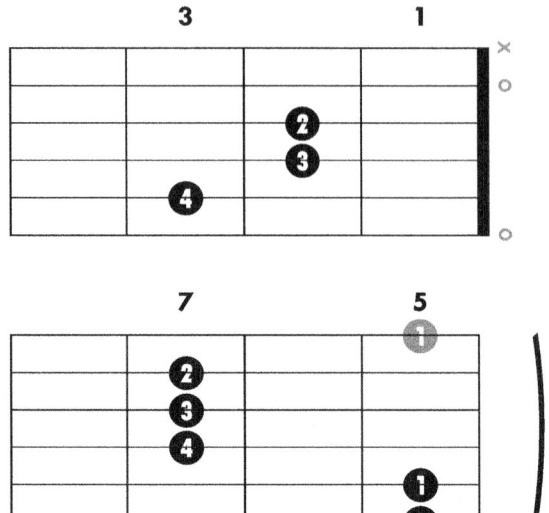

A7sus4

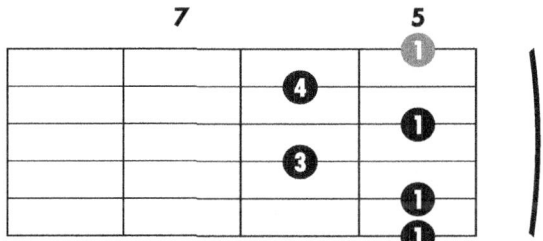

A6/9

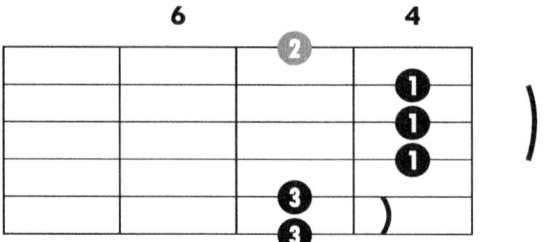

Aaug

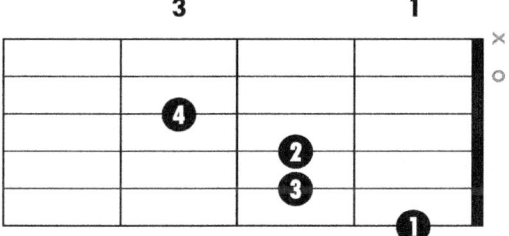

A7#9

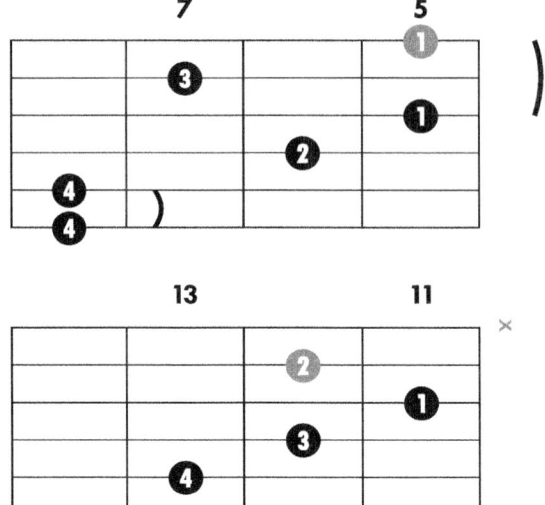

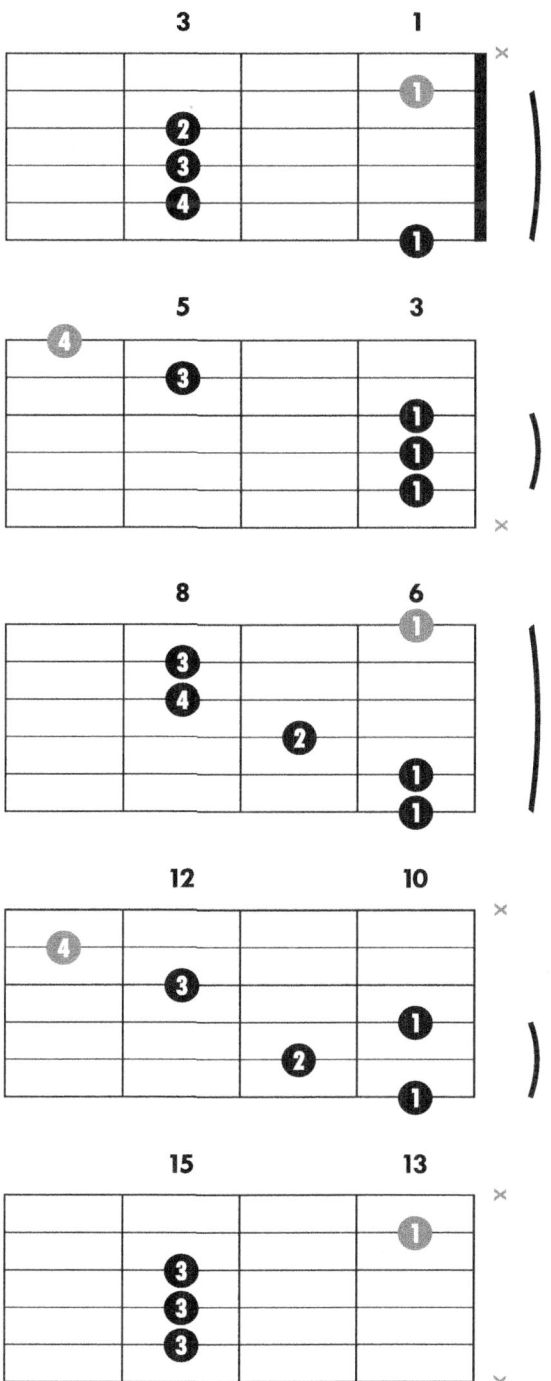

A#
B♭

33

B♭m

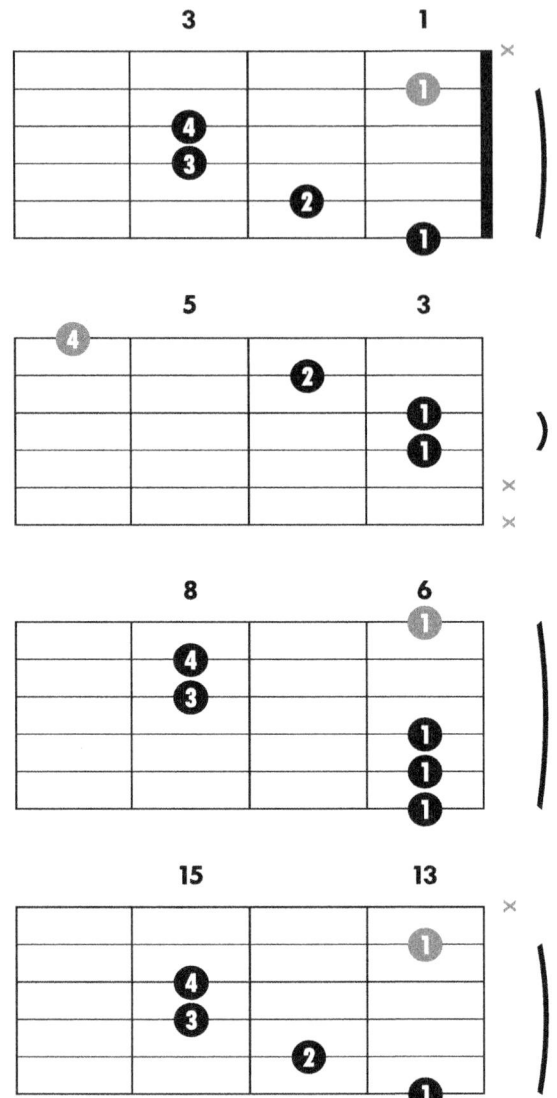

B♭7

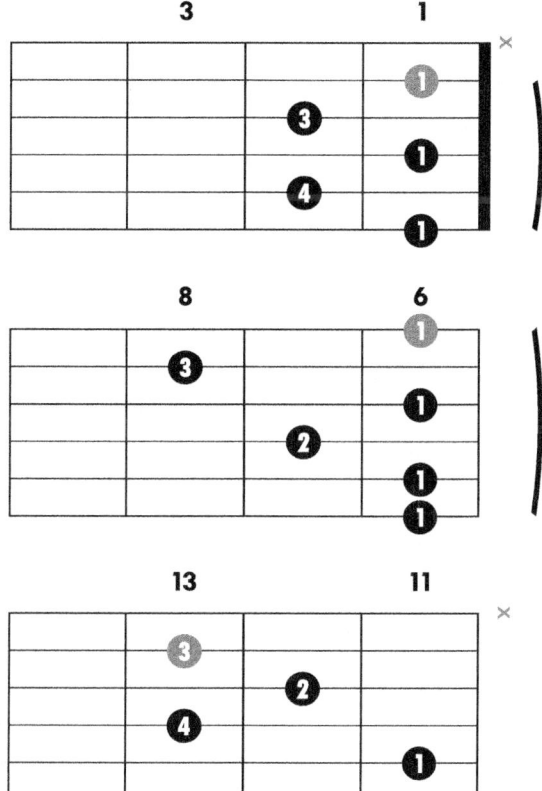

B♭m7

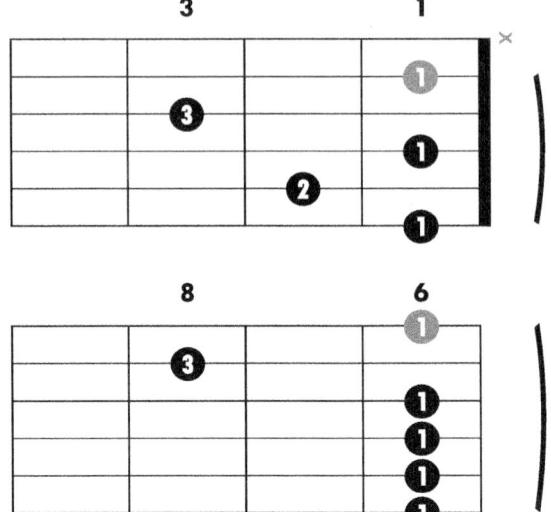

B♭maj7

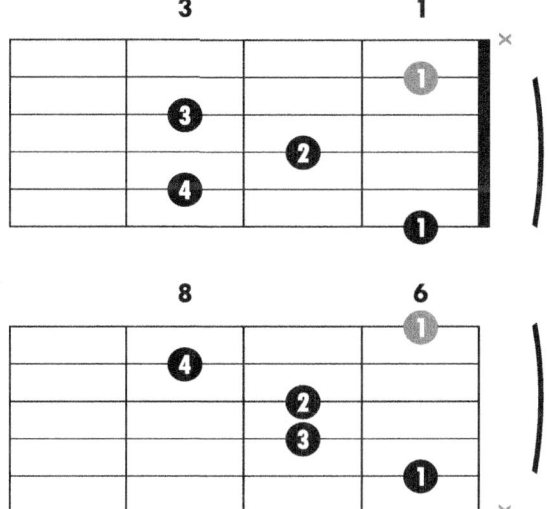

B♭5

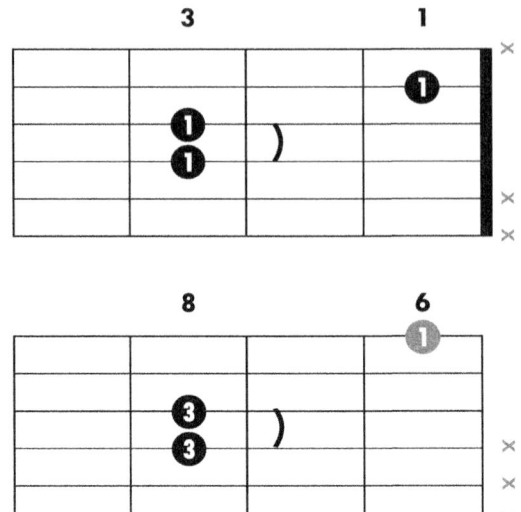

B♭6

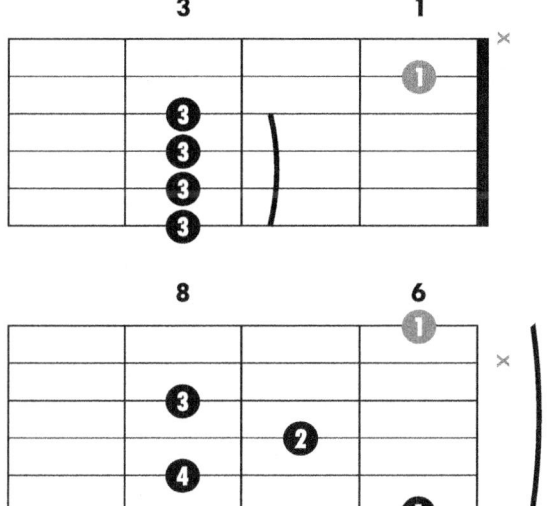

B♭m6

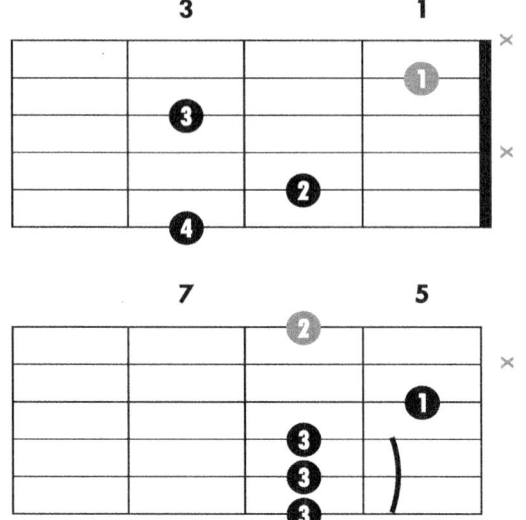

B♭9

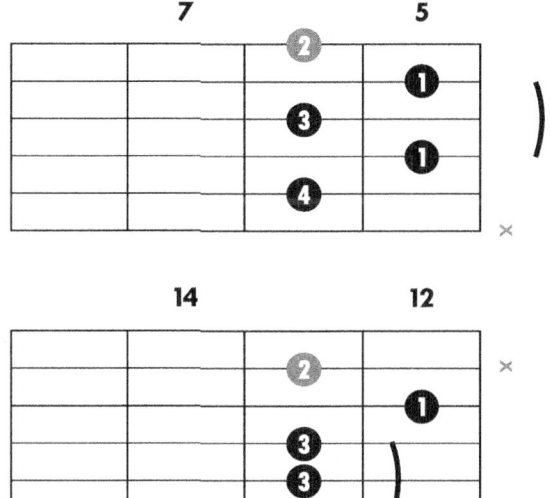

B♭m9

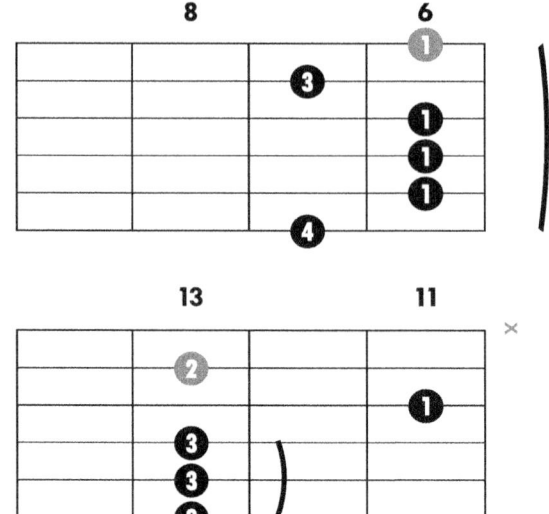

B♭maj9

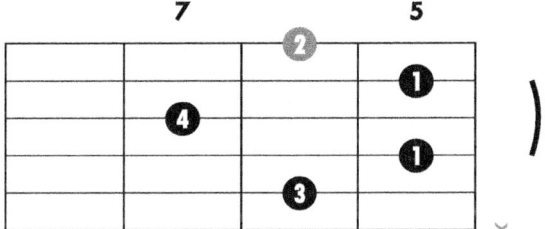

B♭dim7

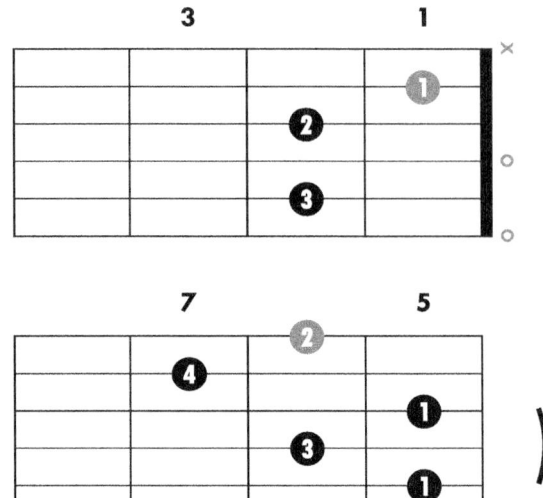

Bb11

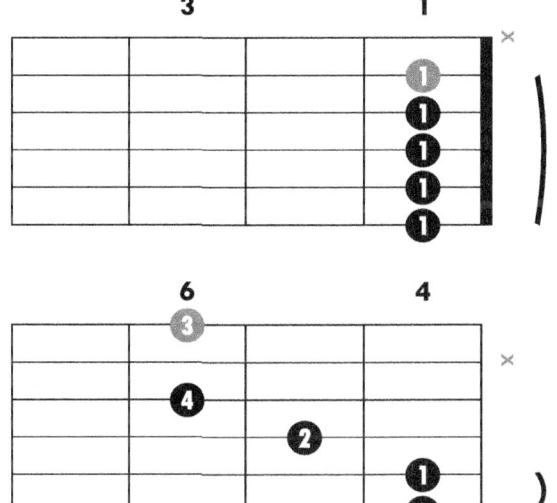

Bb13

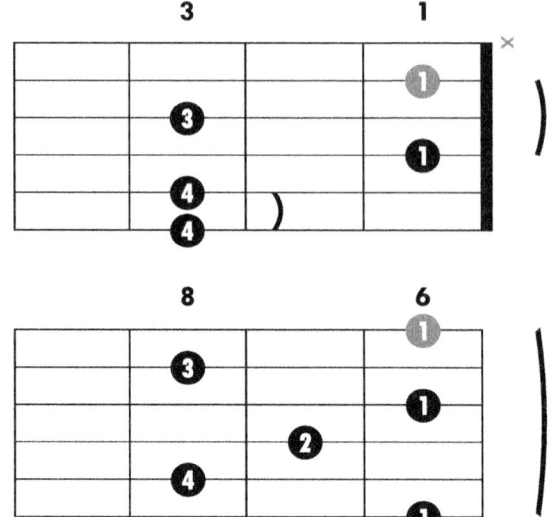

Bbm13

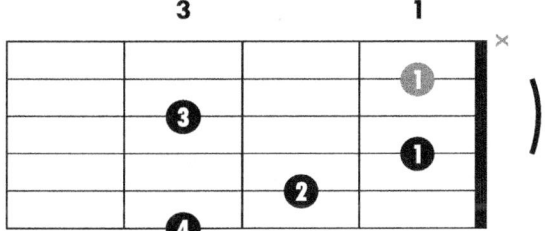

B♭add9

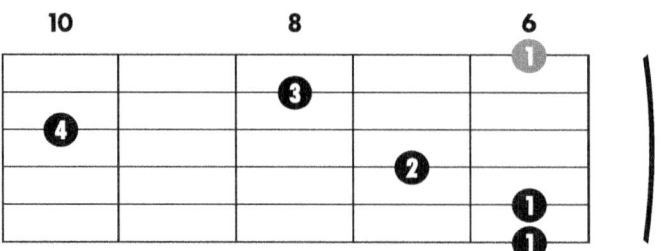

B♭sus4

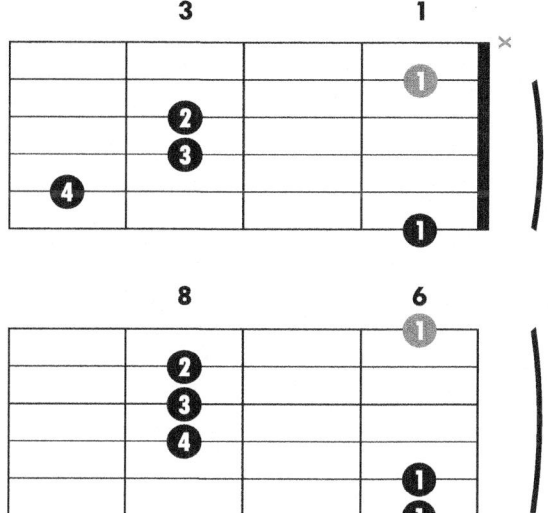

B♭7sus4

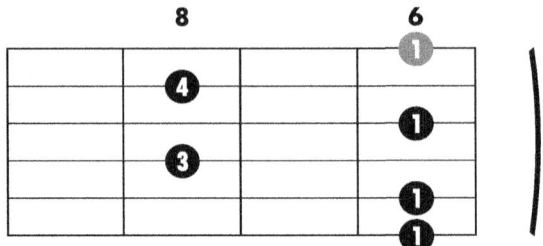

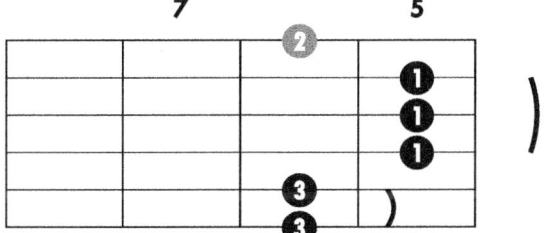

Bb6/9

B♭aug

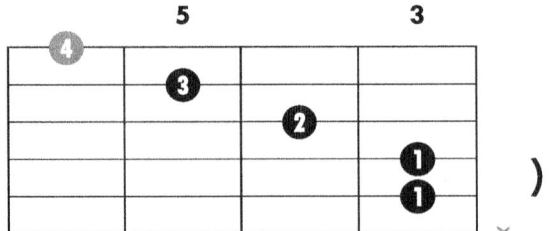

B♭7#9

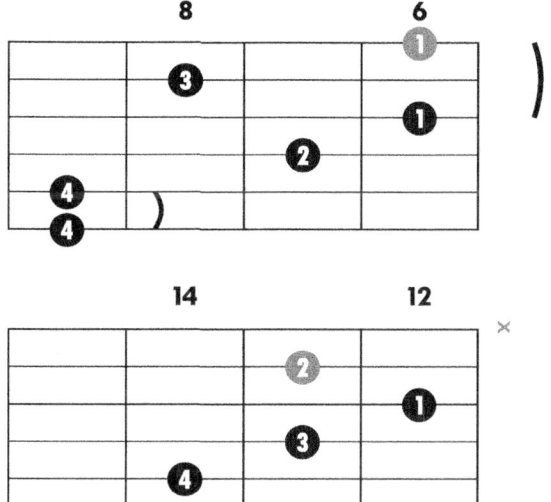

B

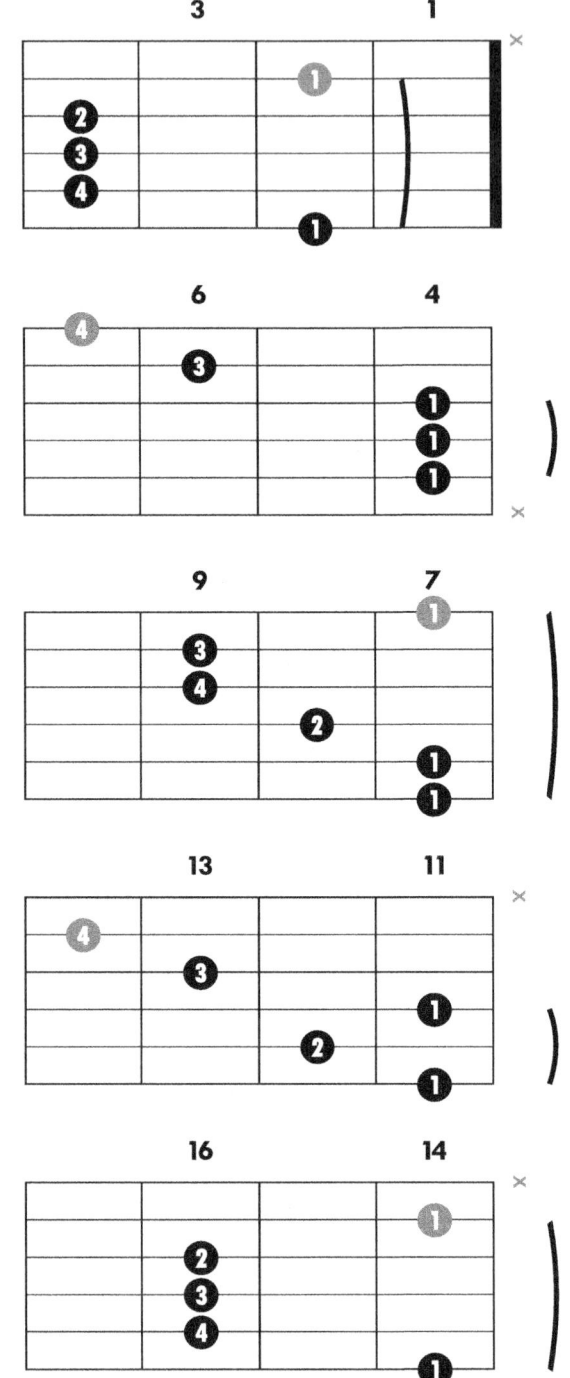

Bm

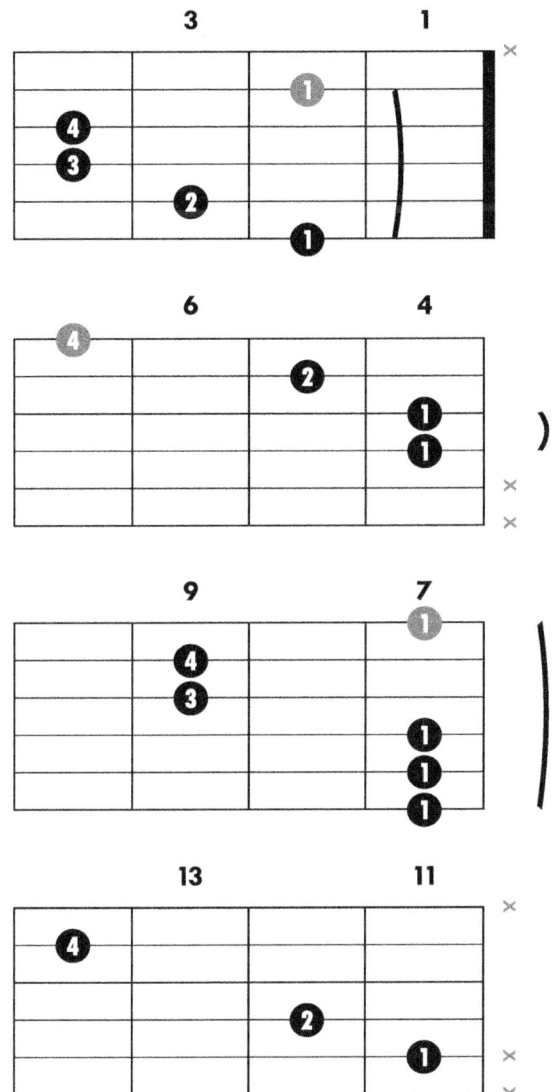

B7

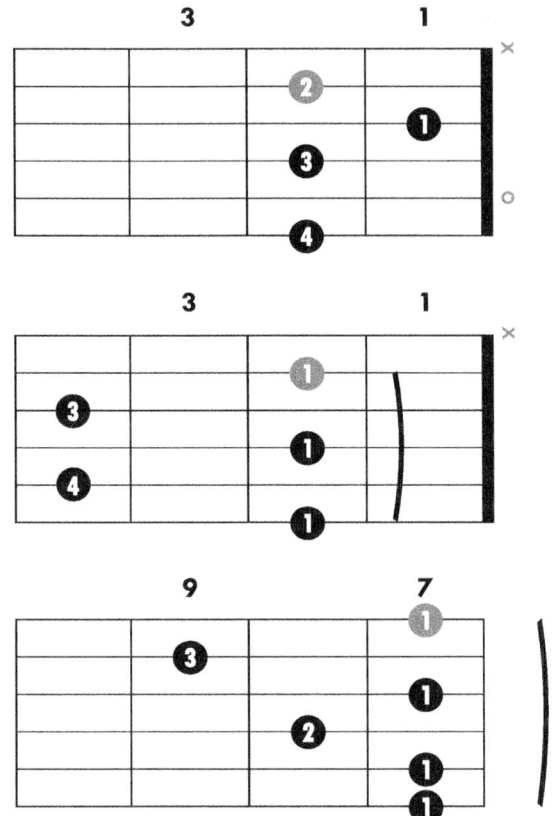

Bm7

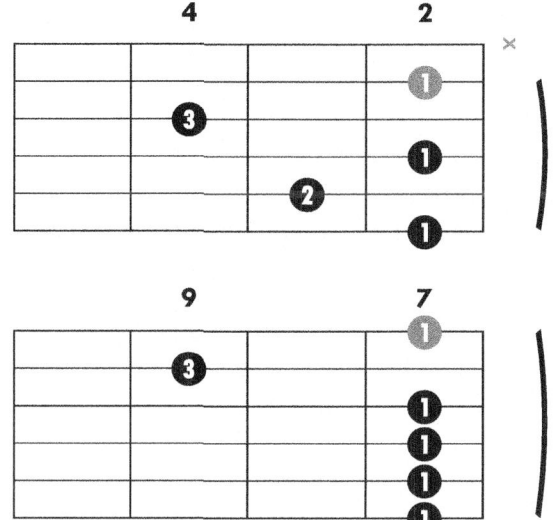

Bmaj7

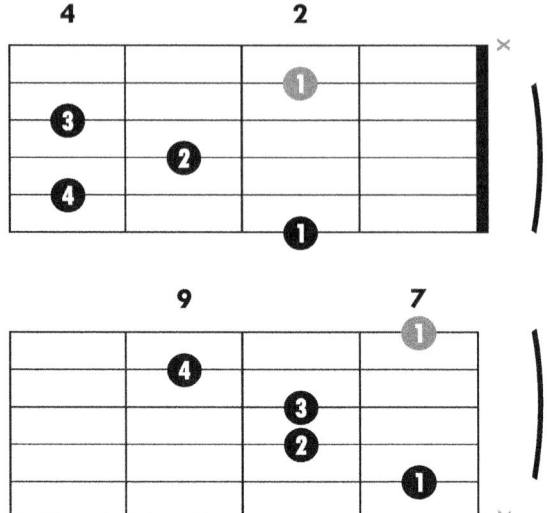

B5

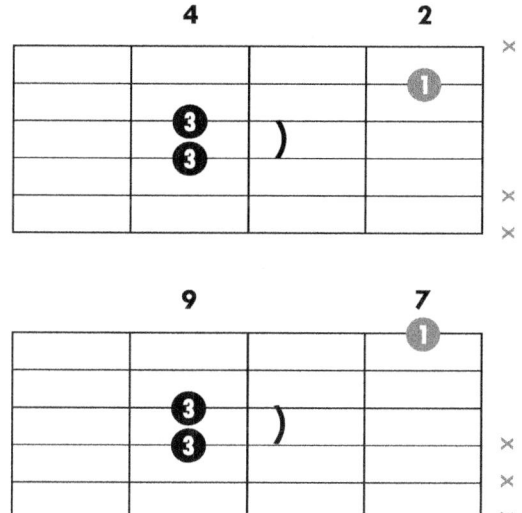

B6

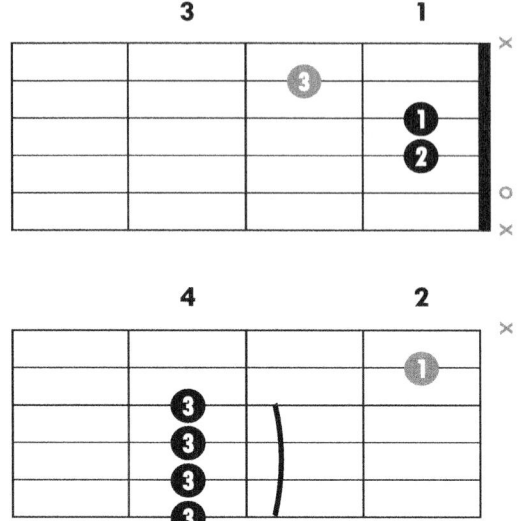

Bm6

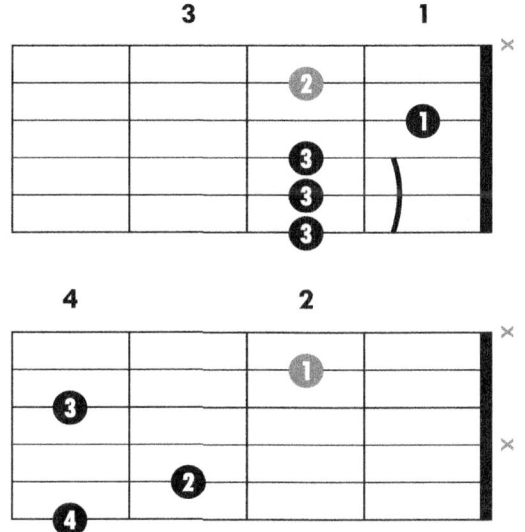

61

B9

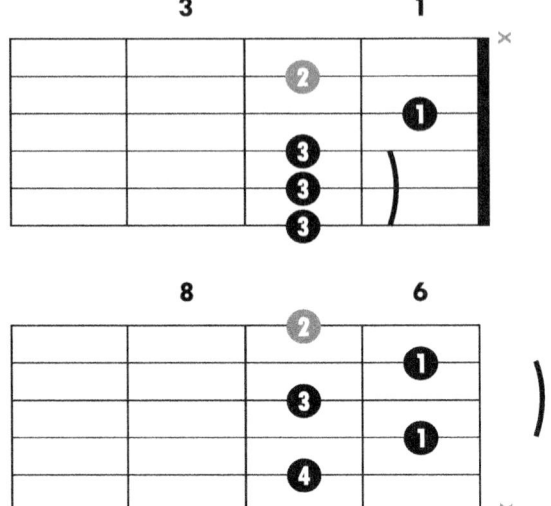

Bm9

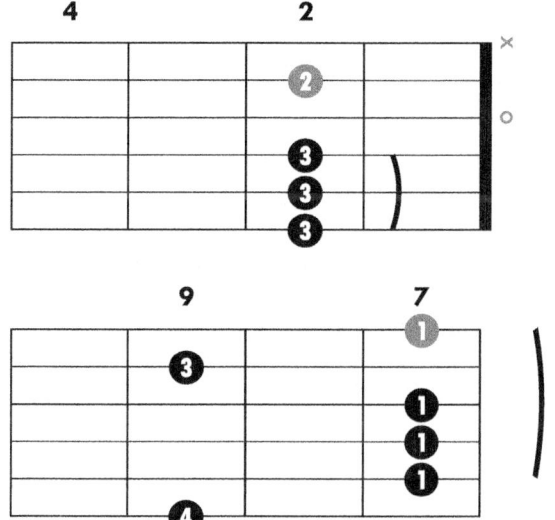

Bmaj9

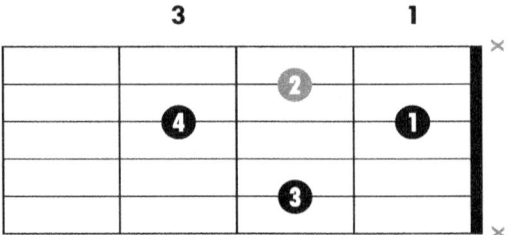

Bdim7

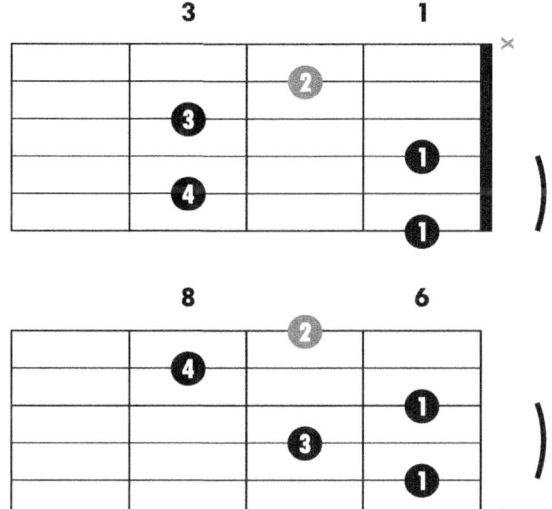

B11

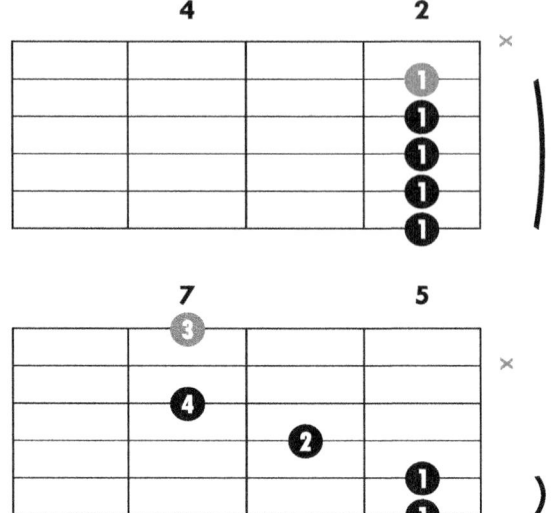

B13

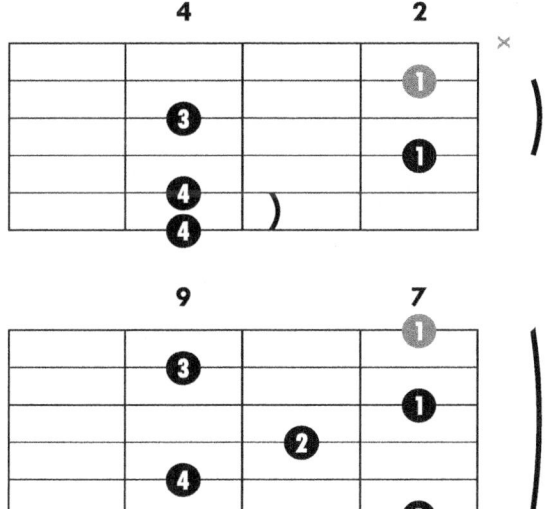

67

Bm13

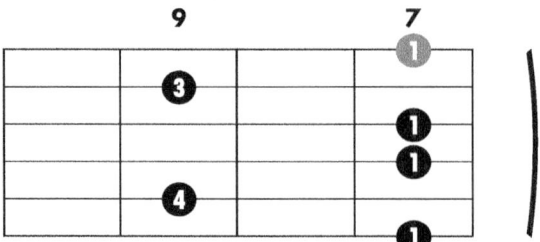

Badd9

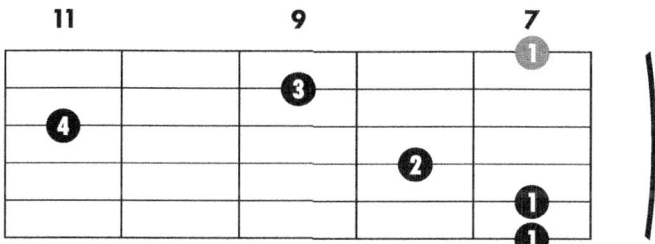

Bsus4

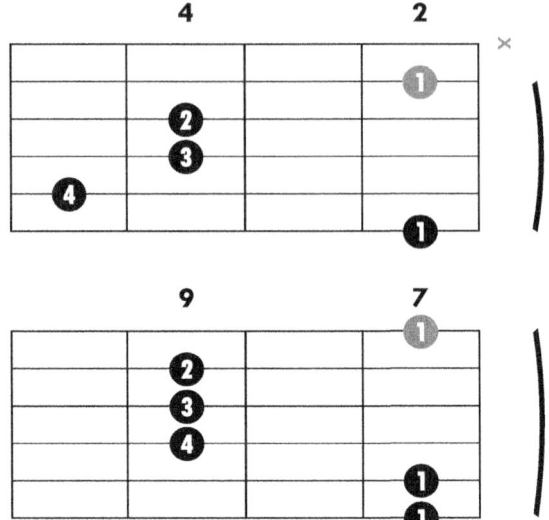

B7sus4

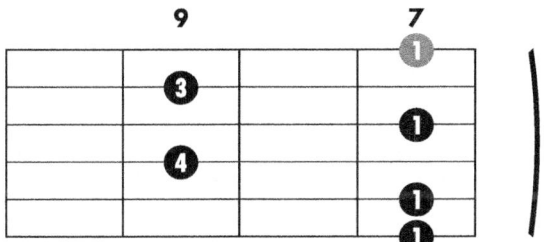

B6/9

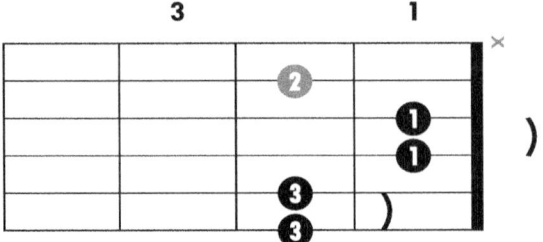

Baug

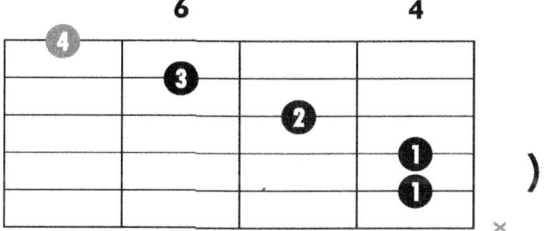

B7#9

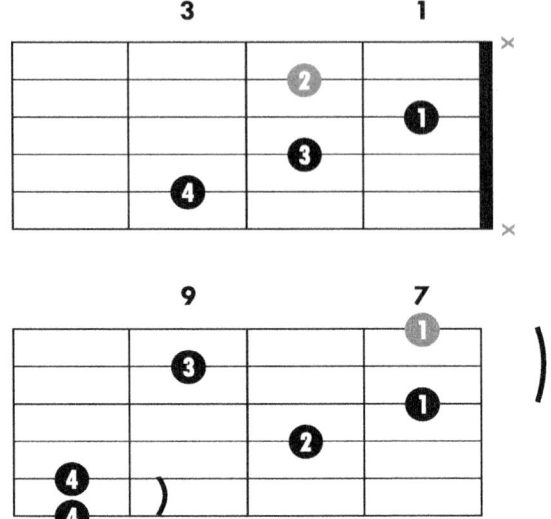

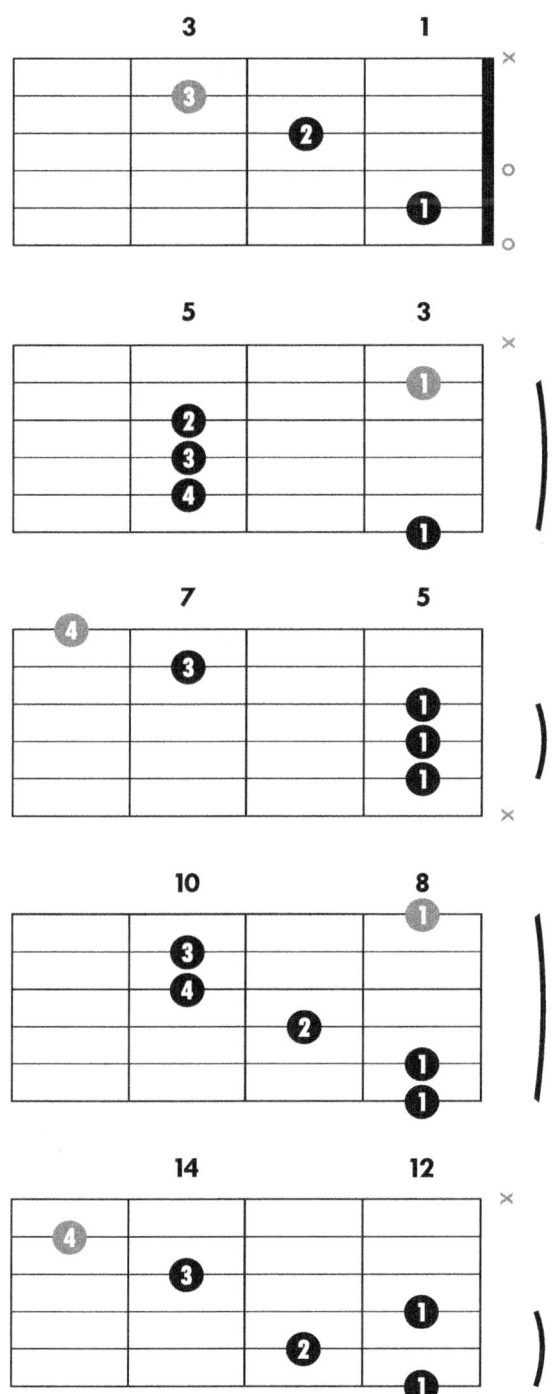

C

Cm

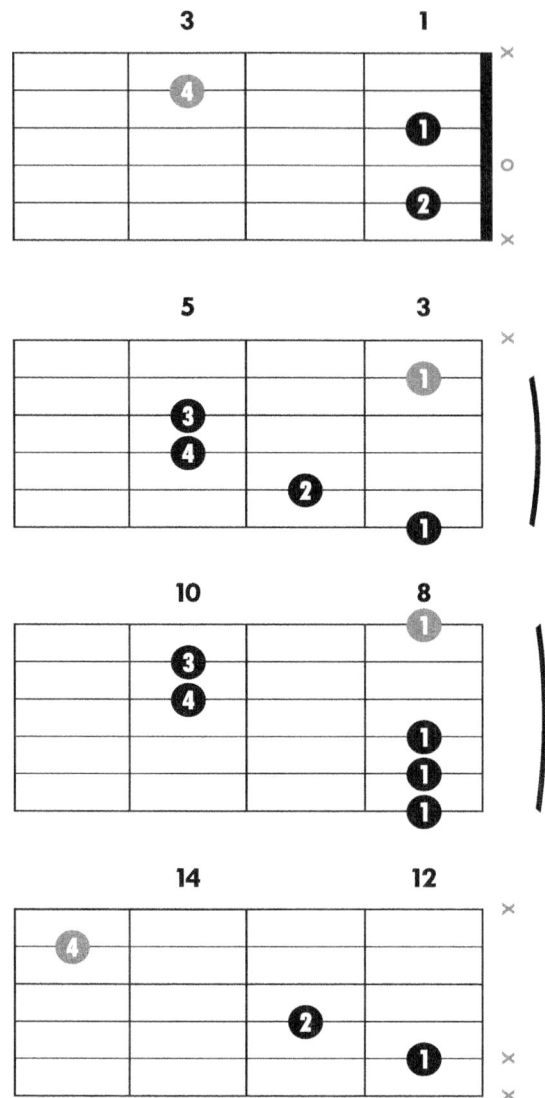

C7

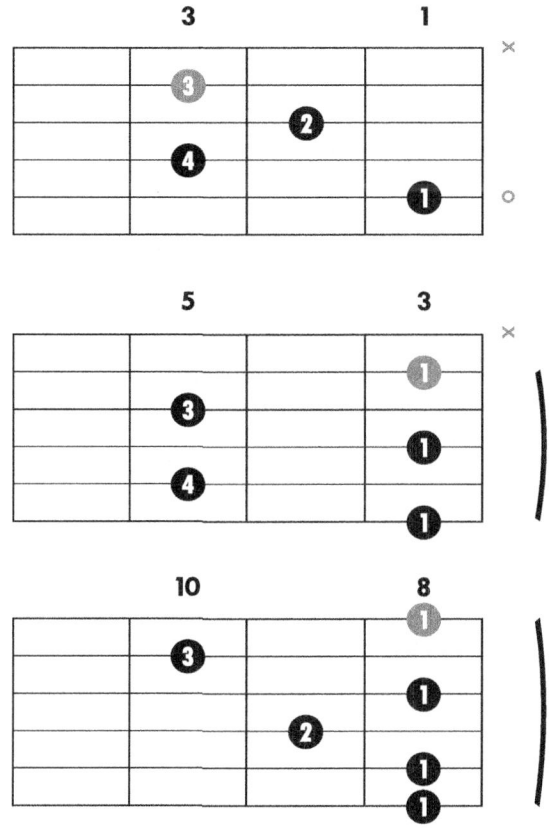

Cm7

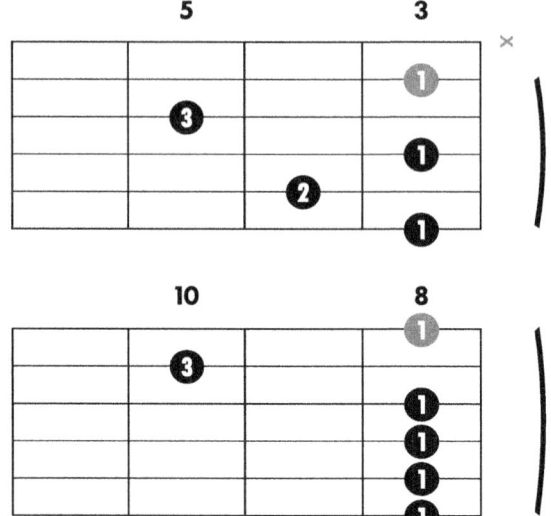

Cmaj7

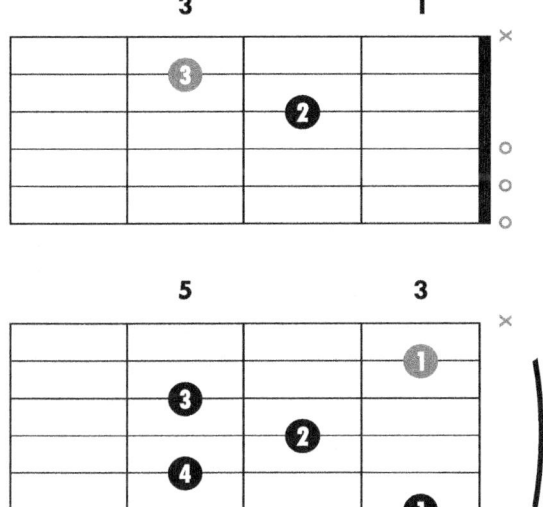

C5

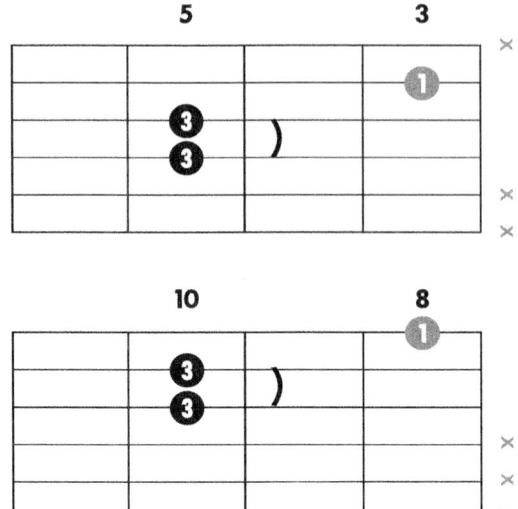

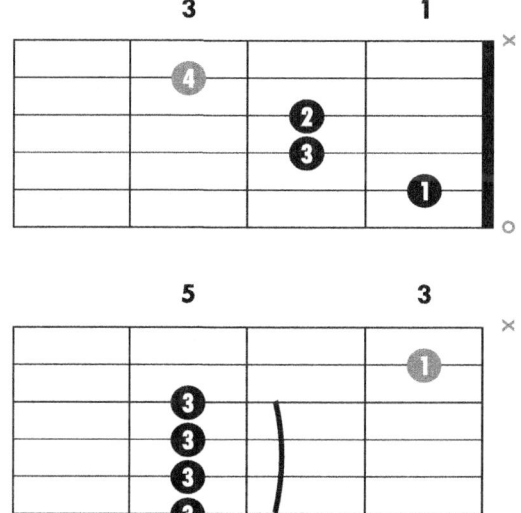

Cm6

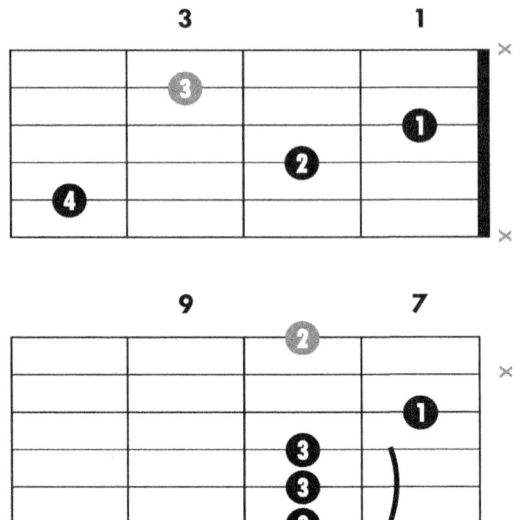

C9

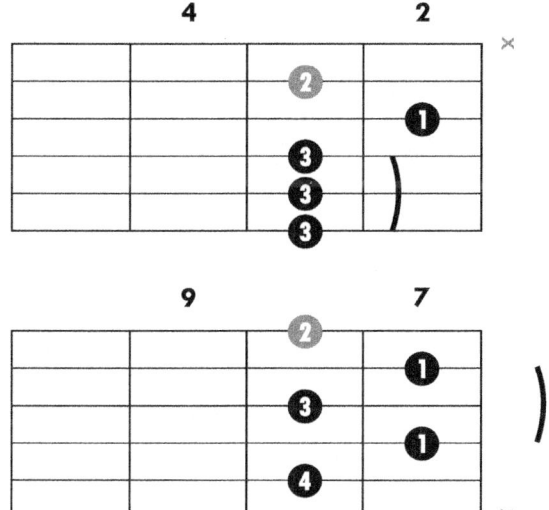

Cm9

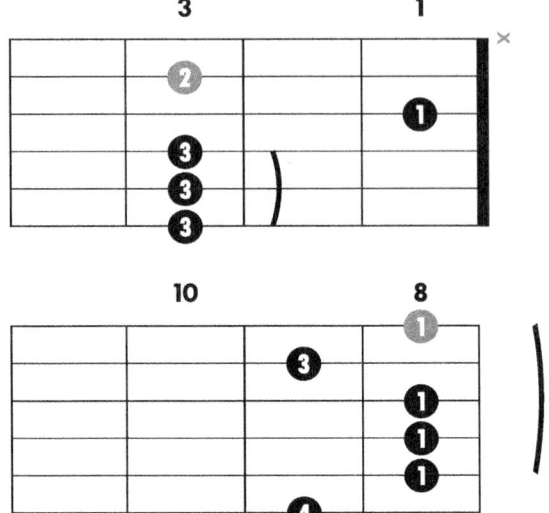

Cmaj9

Cdim7

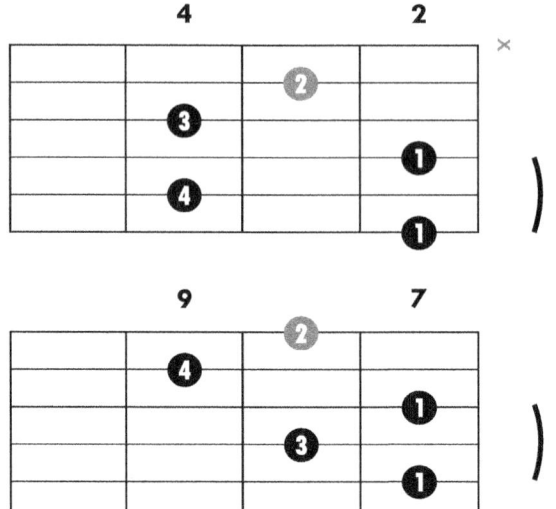

C11

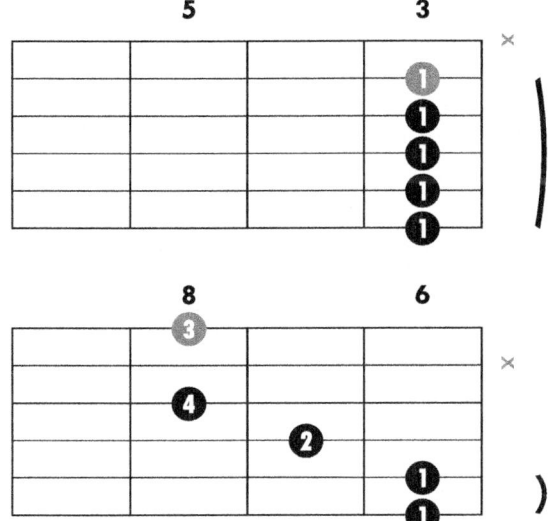

C13

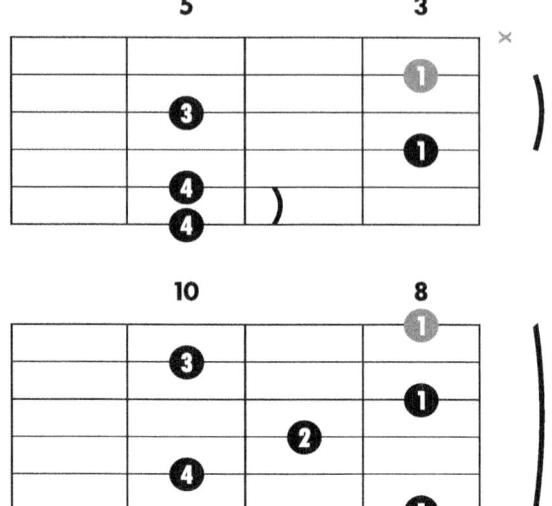

Cm13

Cadd9

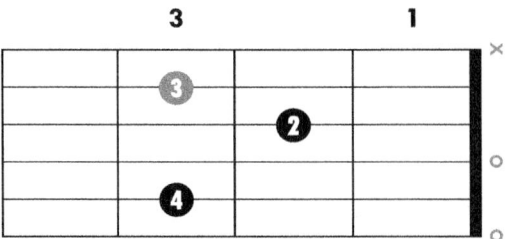

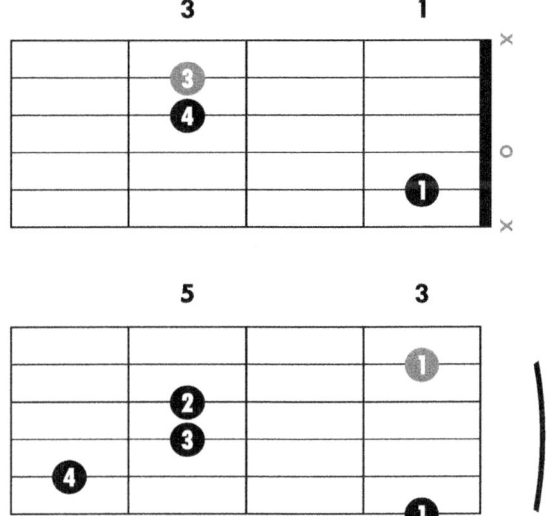

C7sus4

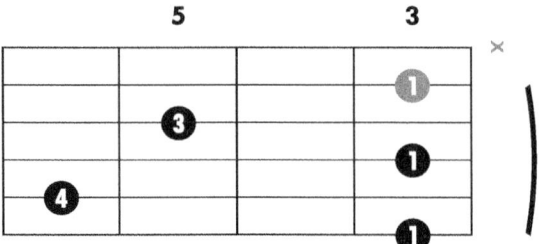

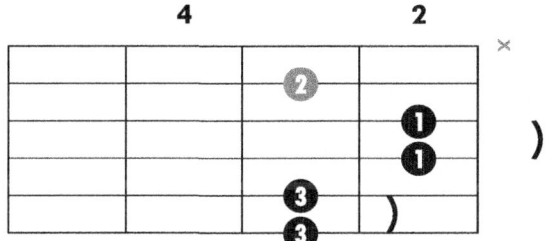

C6/9

Caug

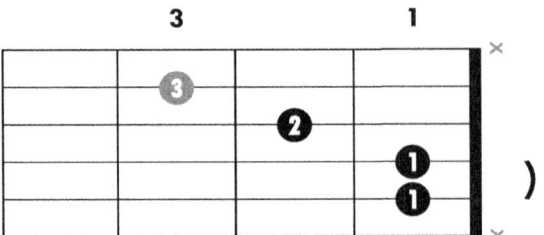

C7#9

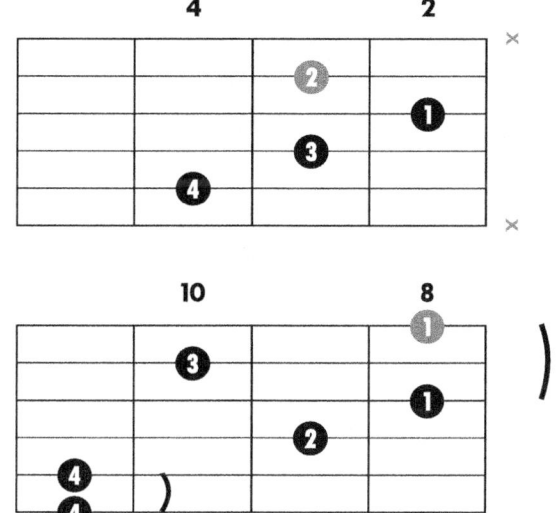

C#
Db

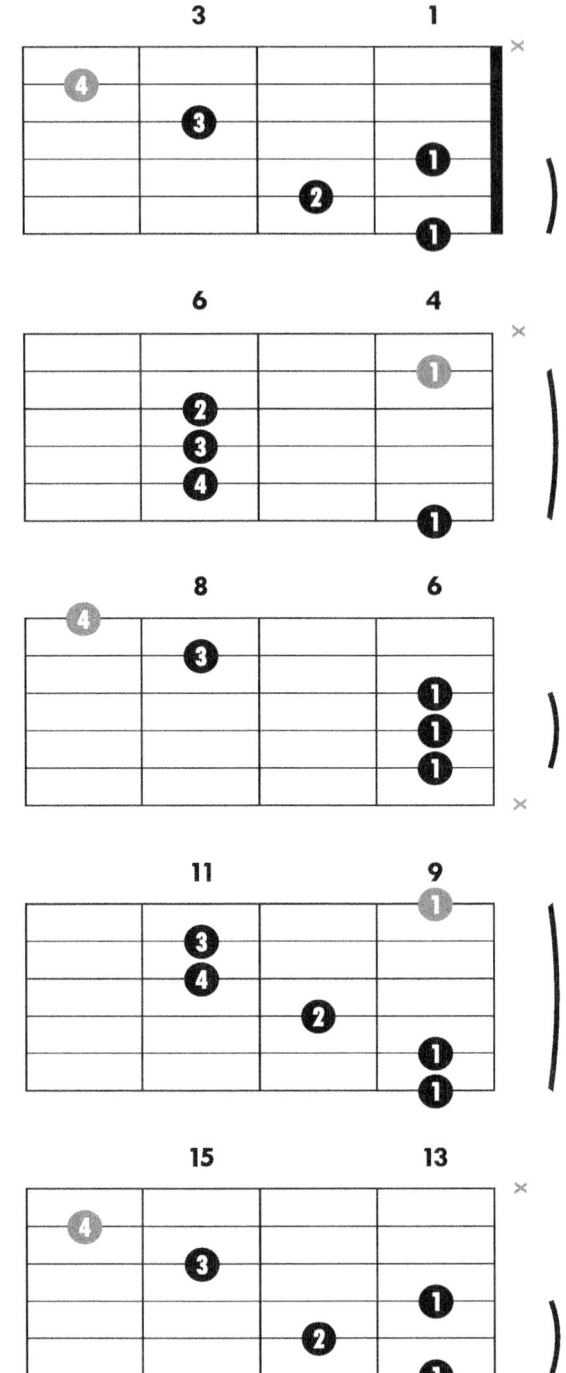

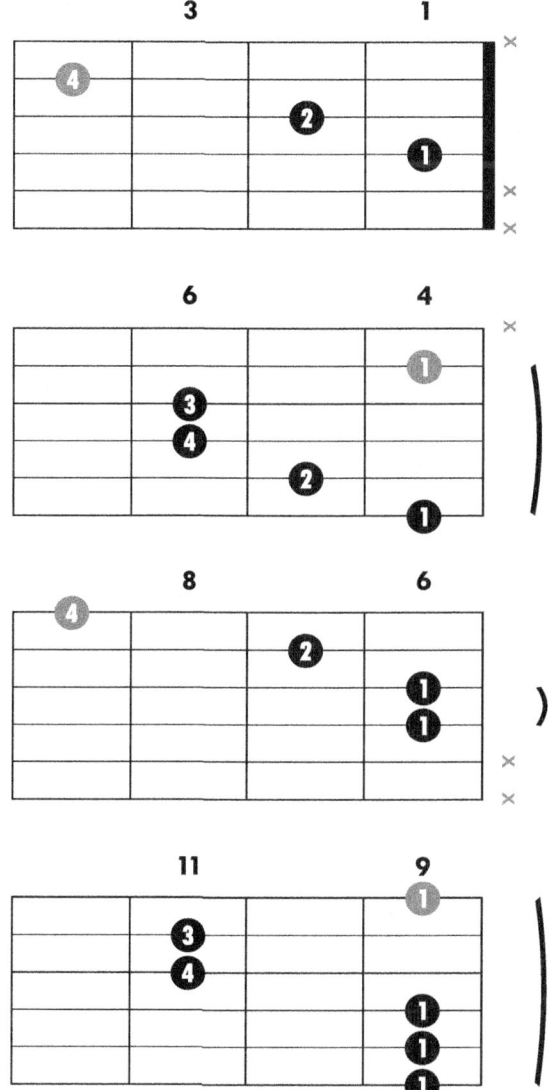

C#7

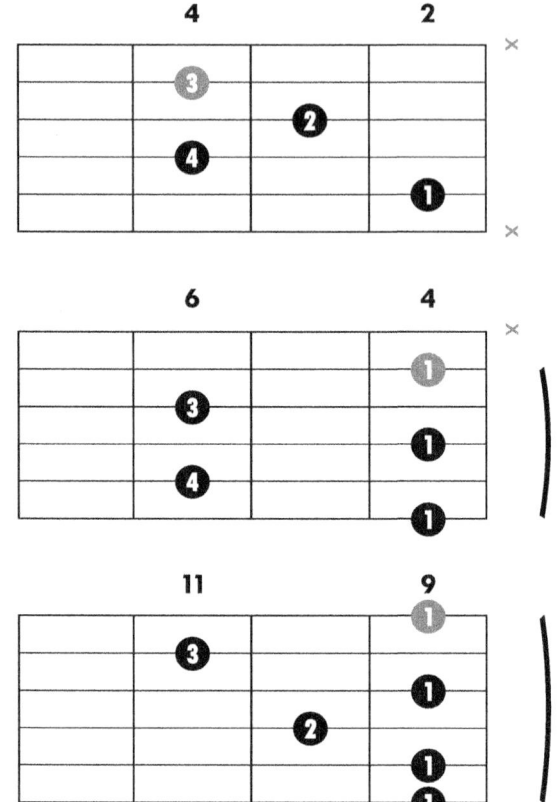

C#m7

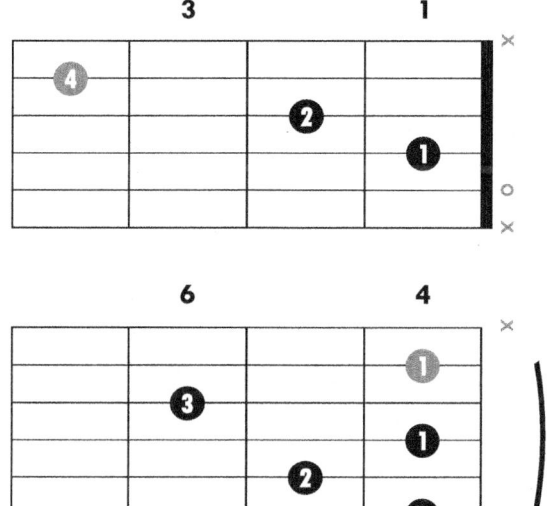

C#maj7

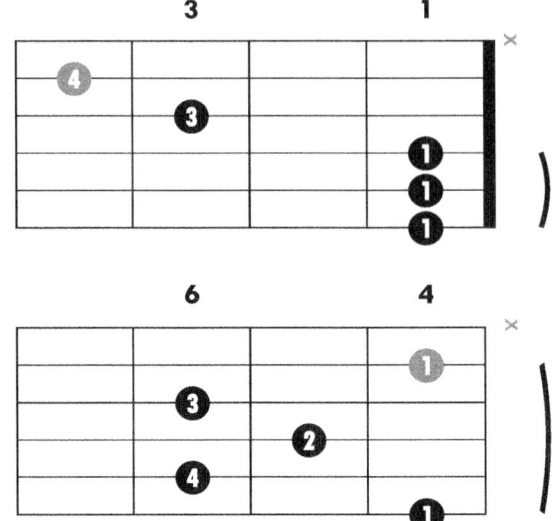

C#5

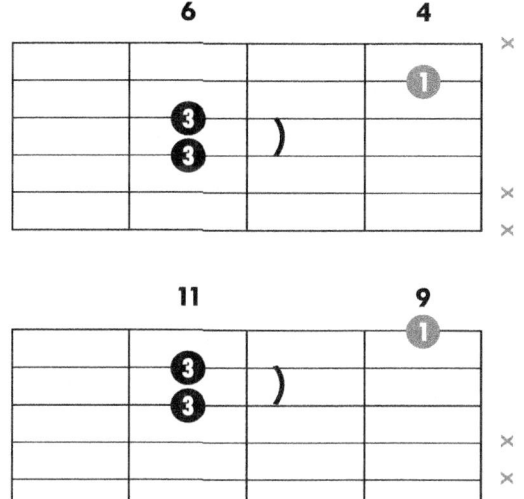

C#6

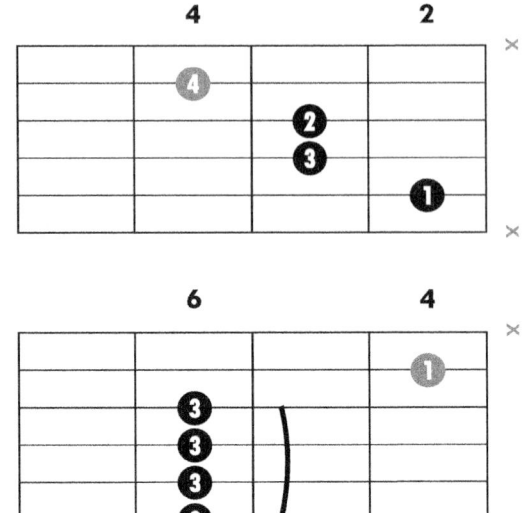

C#m6

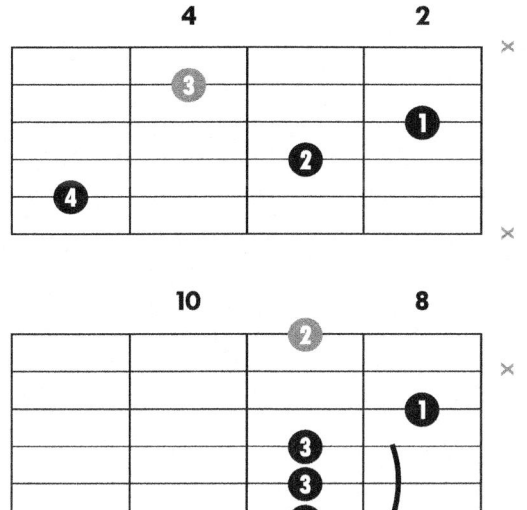

C#9

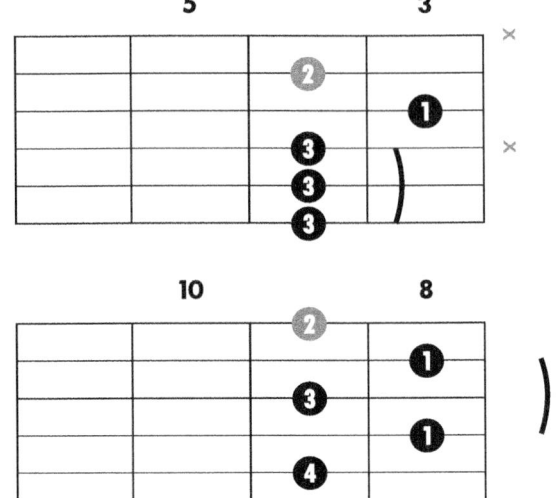

C#m9

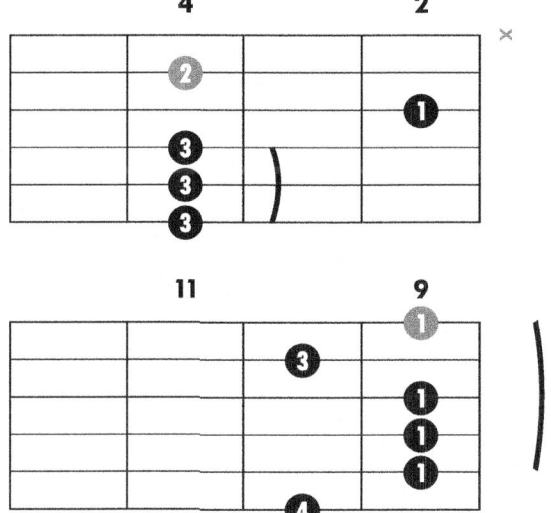

C#maj9

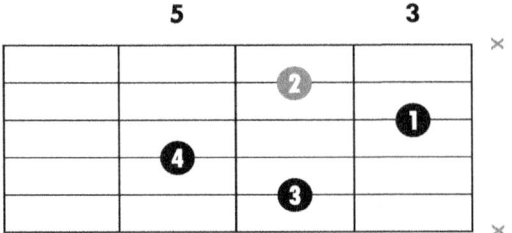

C#dim7

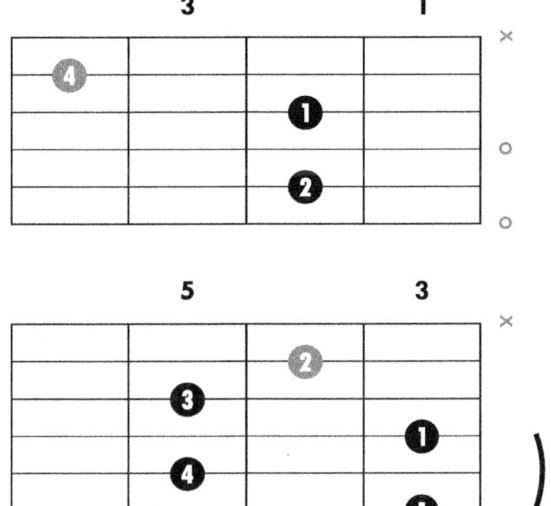

C#11

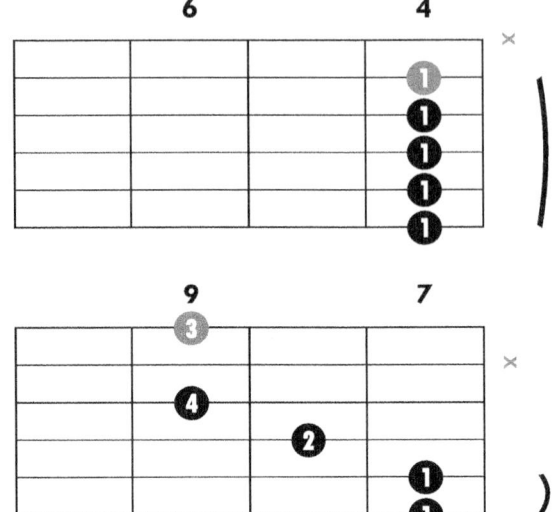

C#13

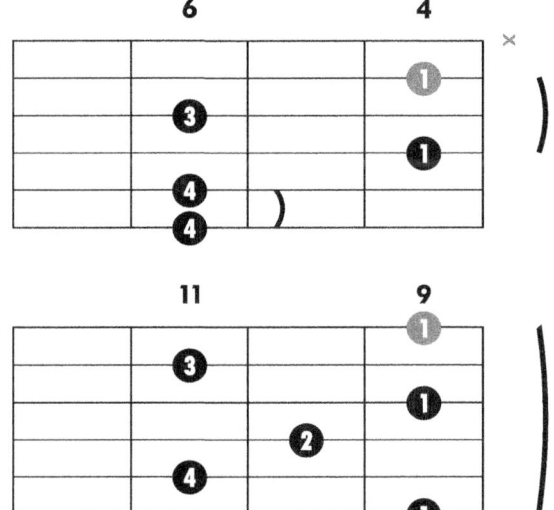

C#m13

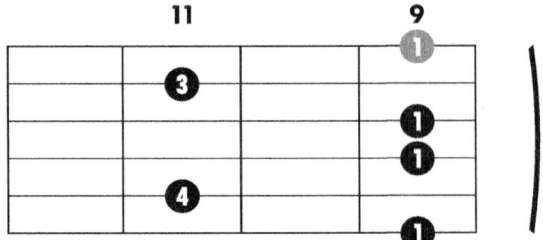

C#add9

C#sus4

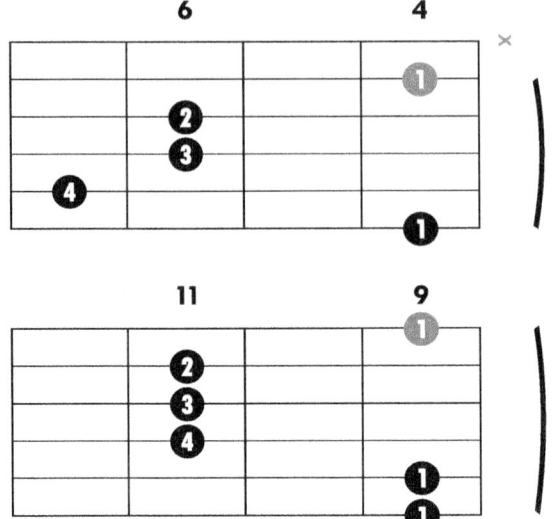

C#7sus4

C#6/9

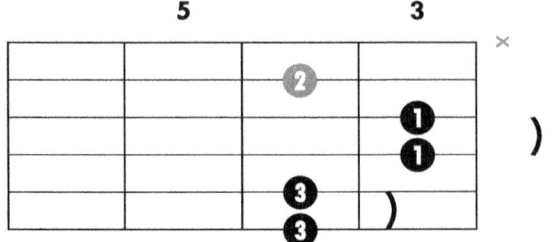

C#aug

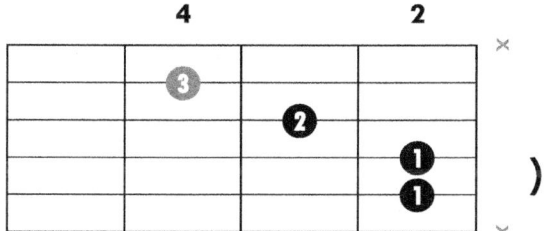

C#7#9

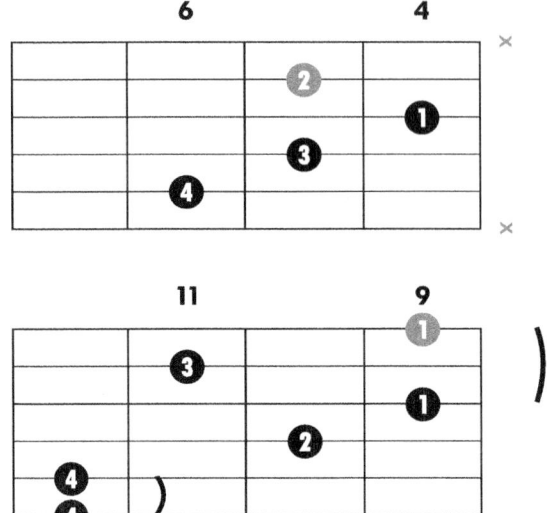

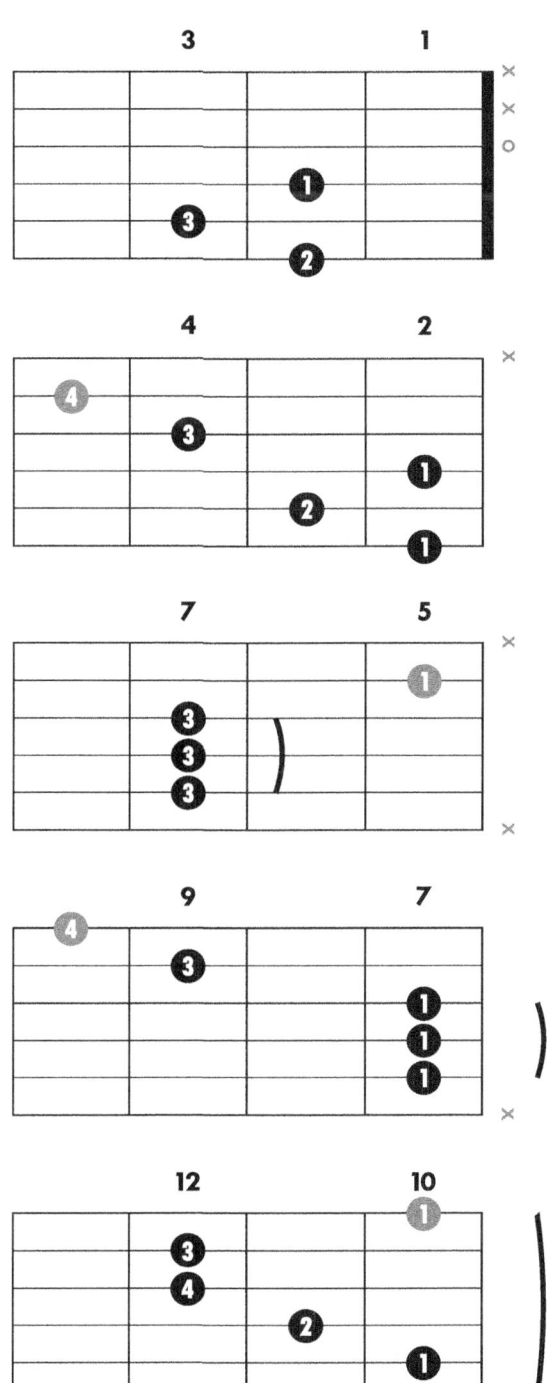

D

Dm

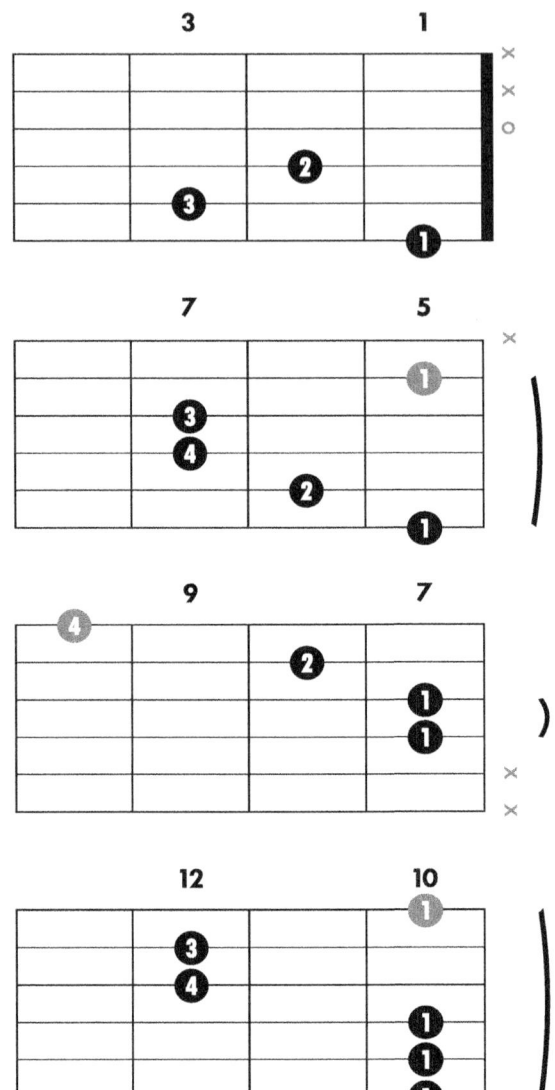

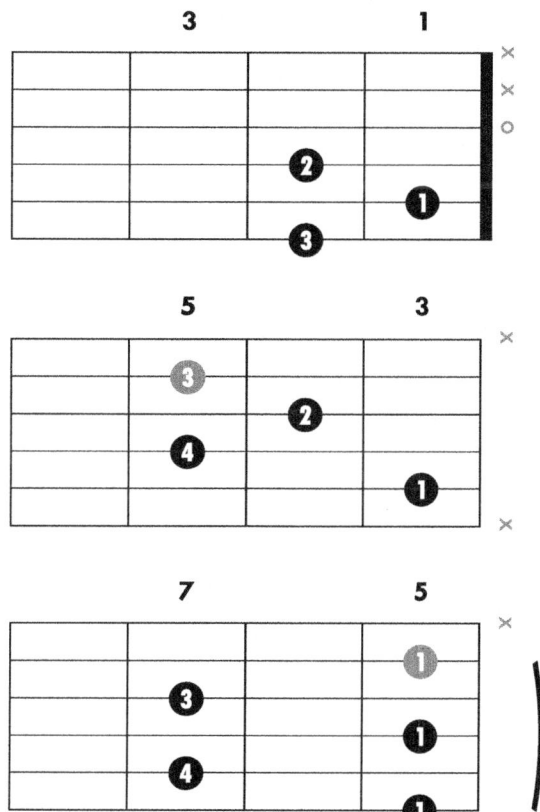

Dm7

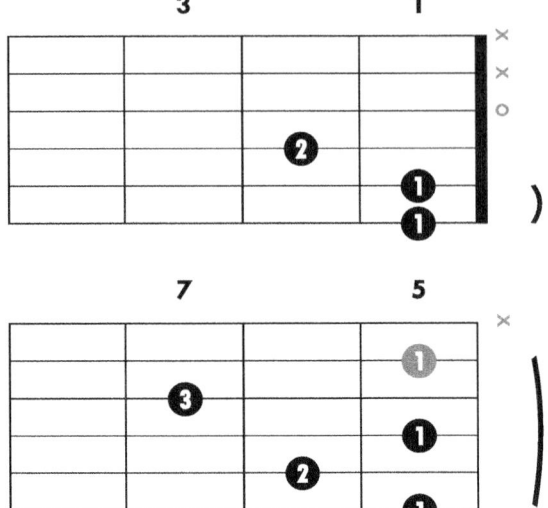

Dmaj7

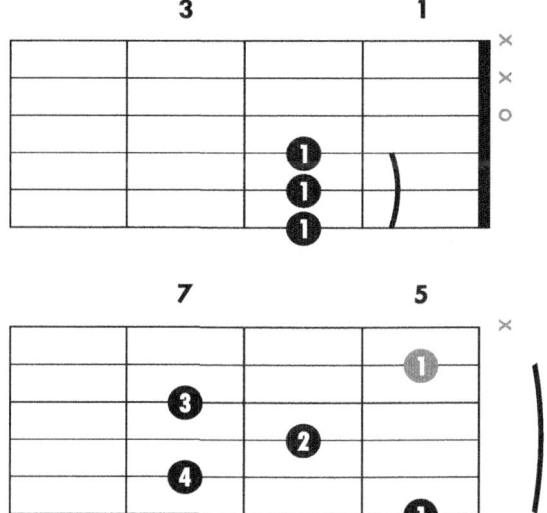

D5

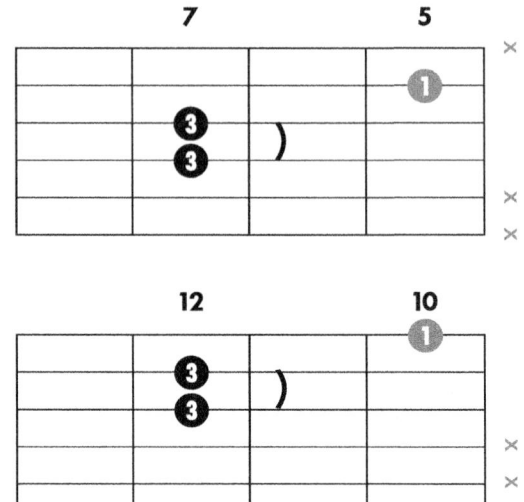

D6

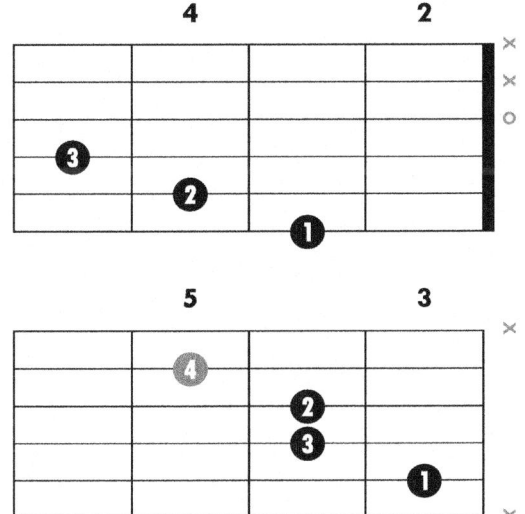

Dm6

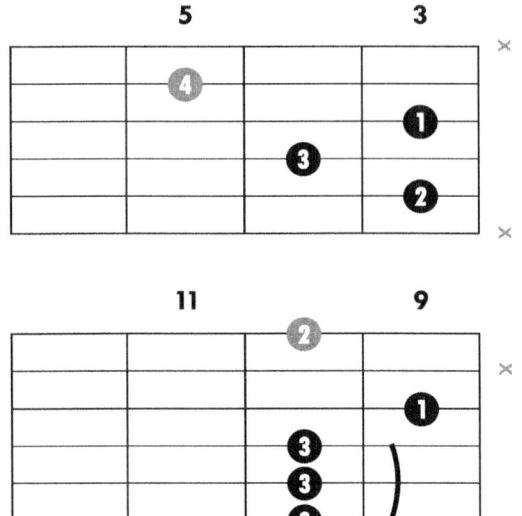

D9

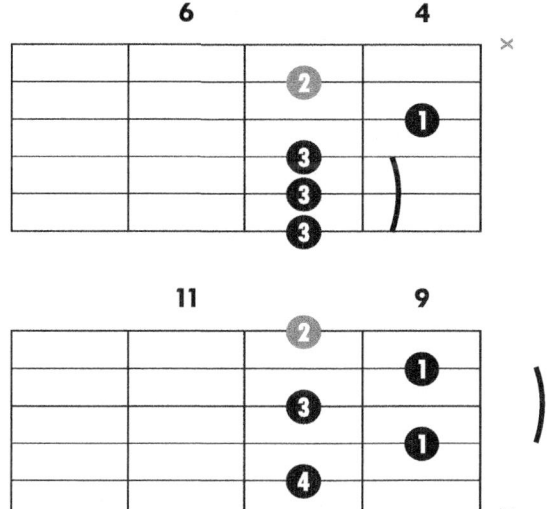

Dm9

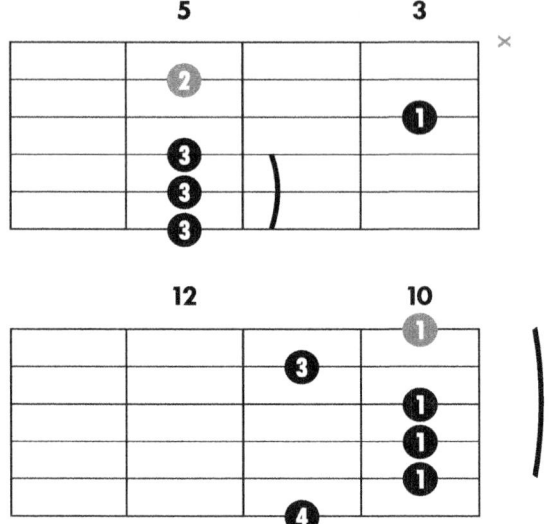

Dmaj9

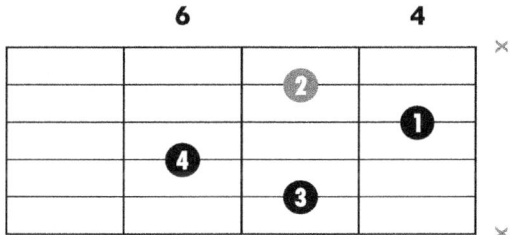

Ddim7

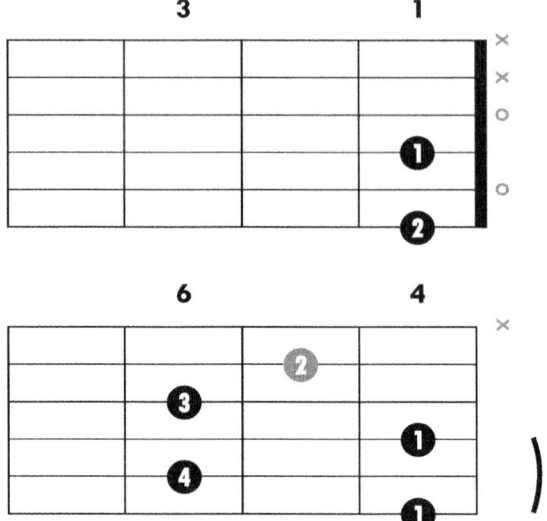

D11

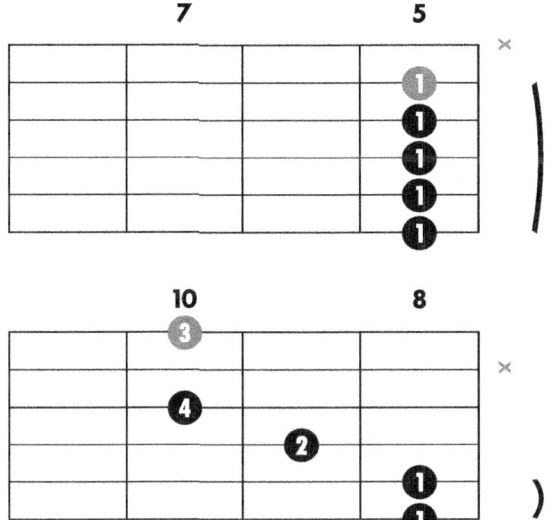

D13

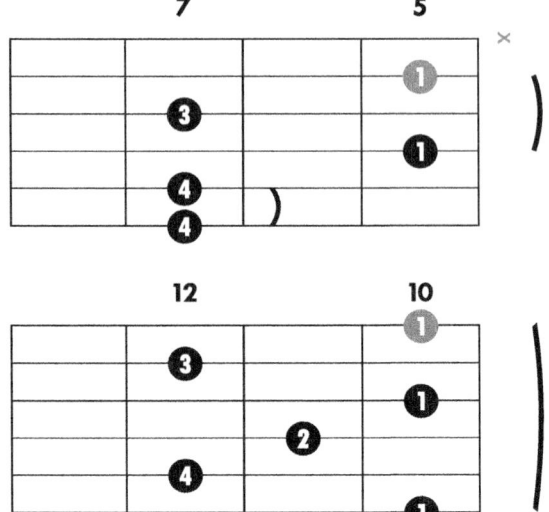

Dm13

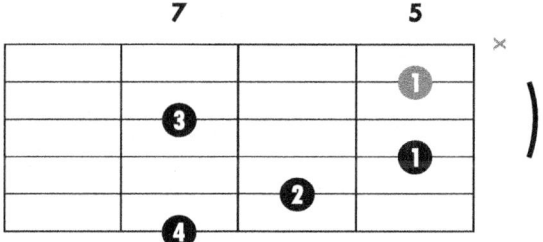

Dadd9

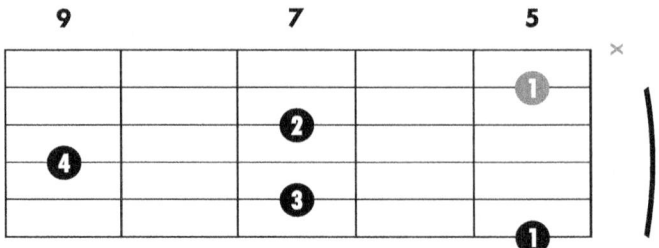

Dsus4

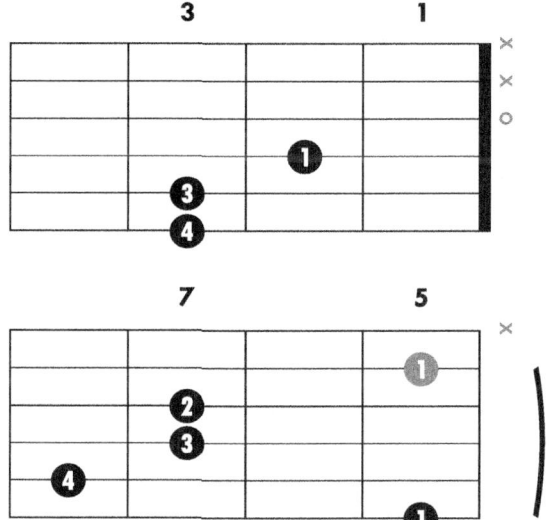

D7sus4

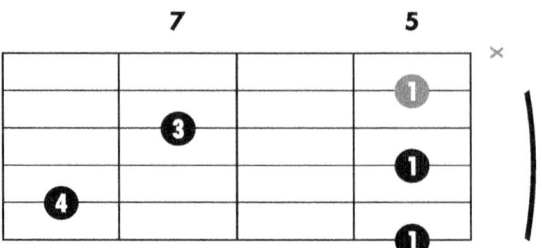

D6/9

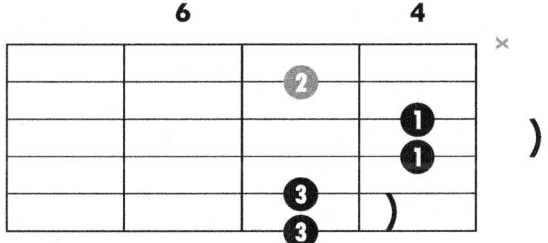

Daug

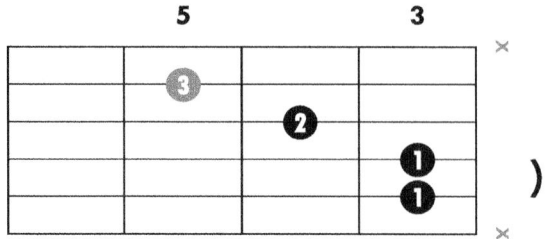

D7#9

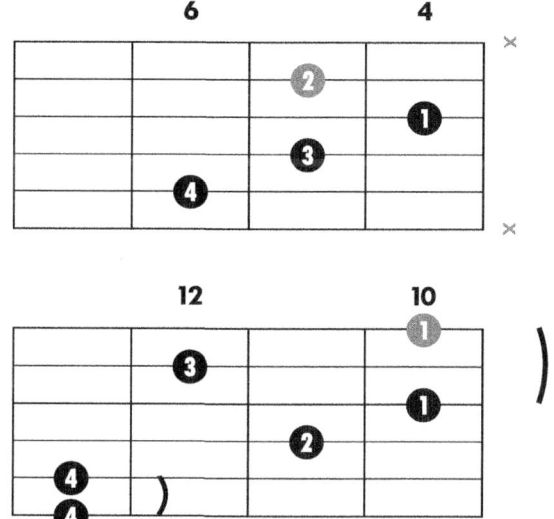

D#
E♭

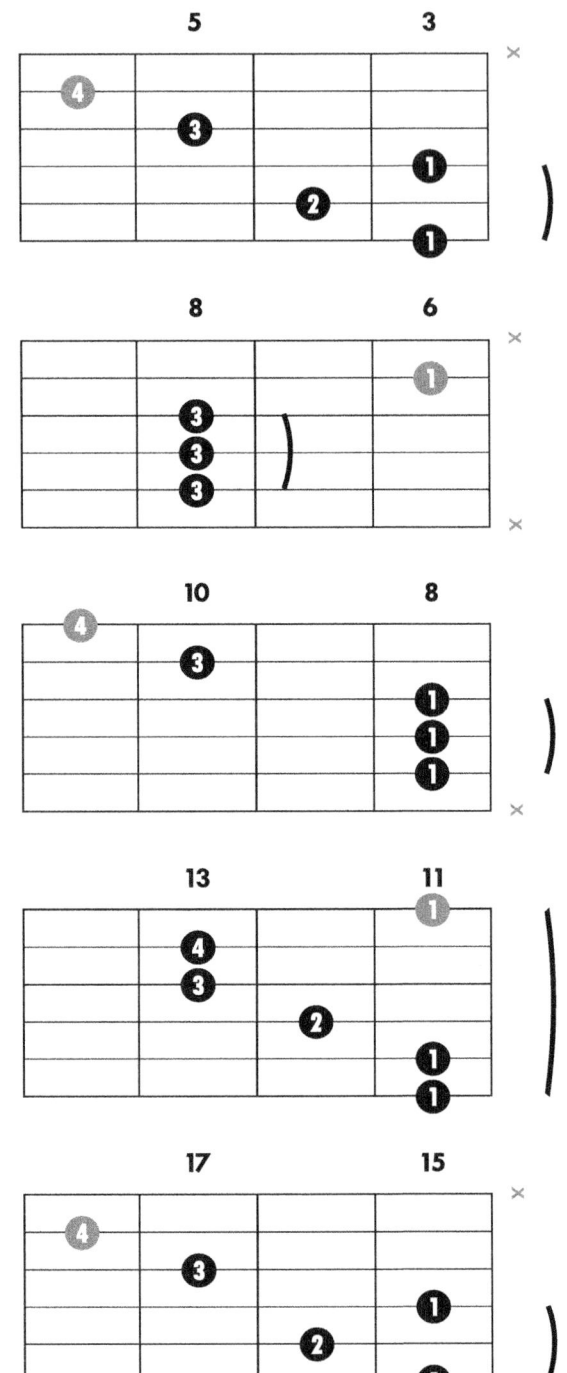

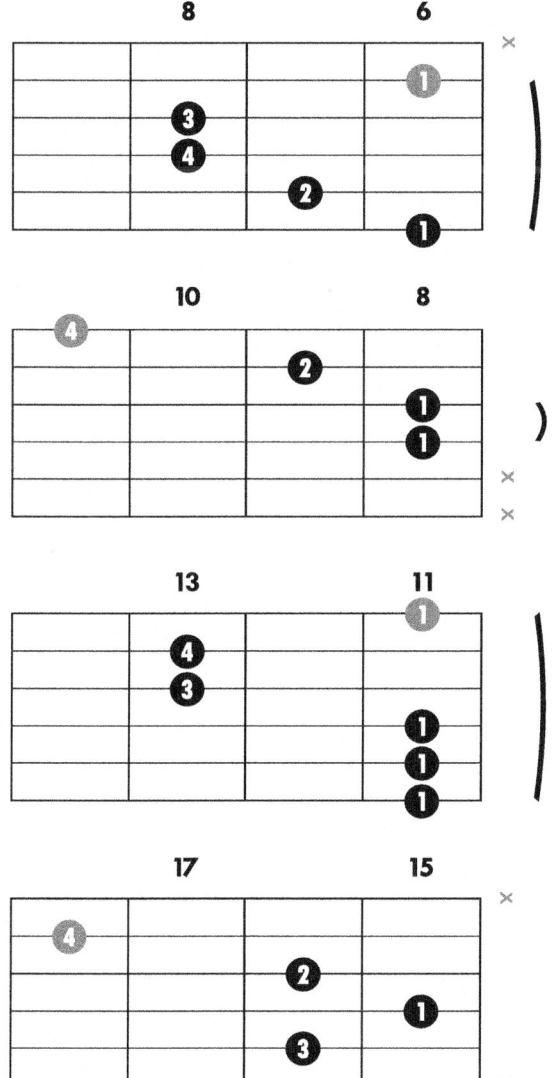

E♭7

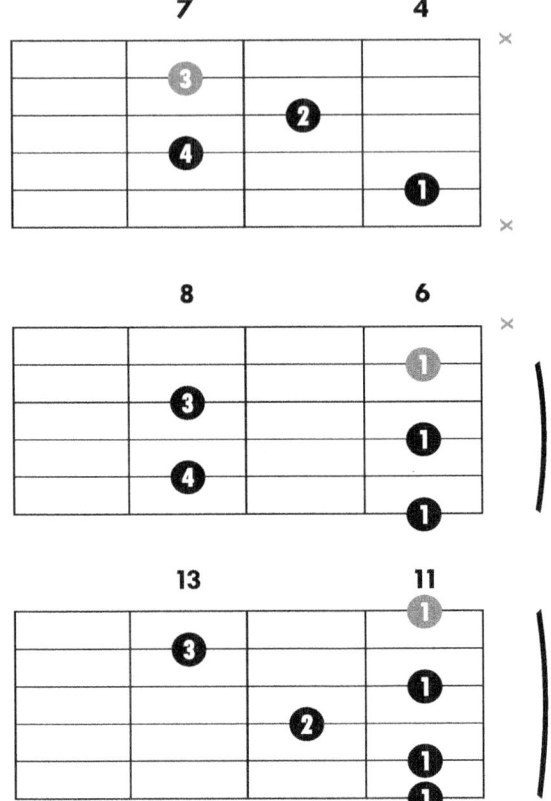

Ebm7

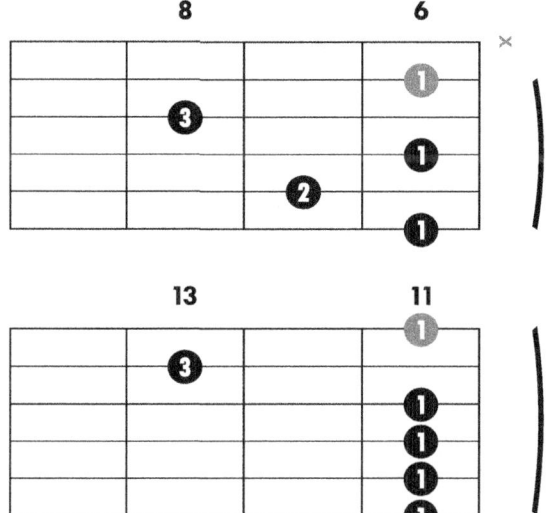

E♭maj7

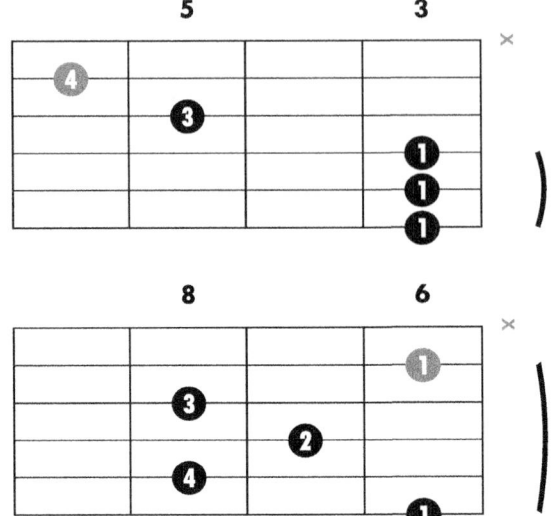

E♭5

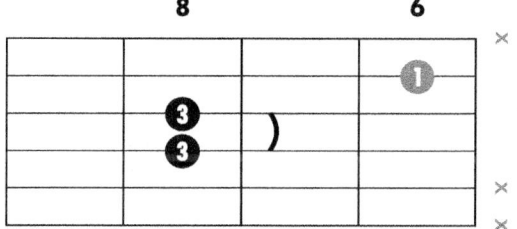

E♭6

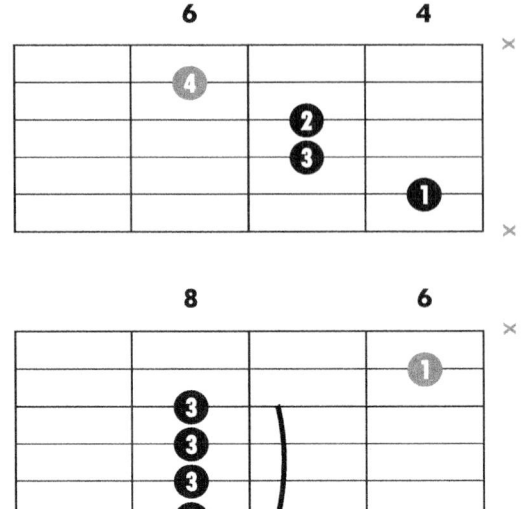

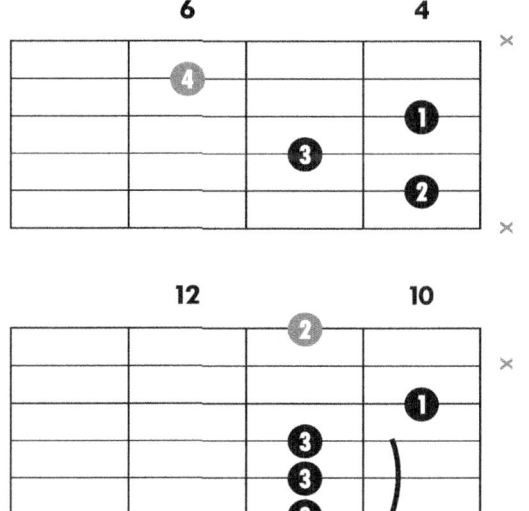

E♭9

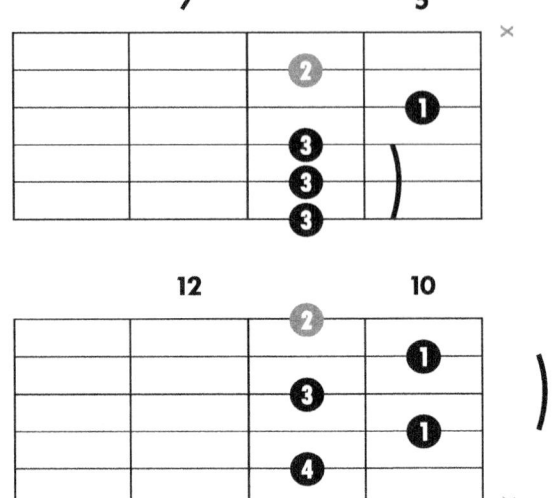

E♭m9

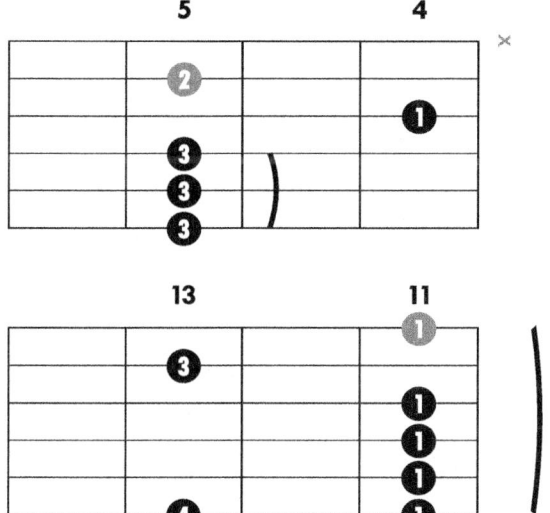

E♭maj9

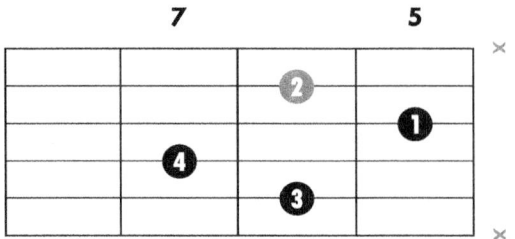

E♭dim7

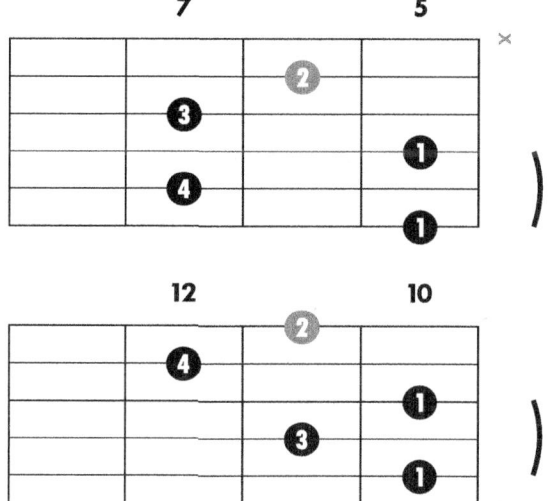

E♭11

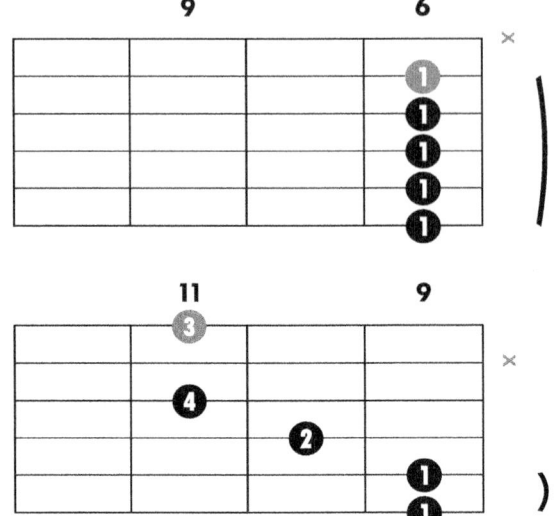

E♭13

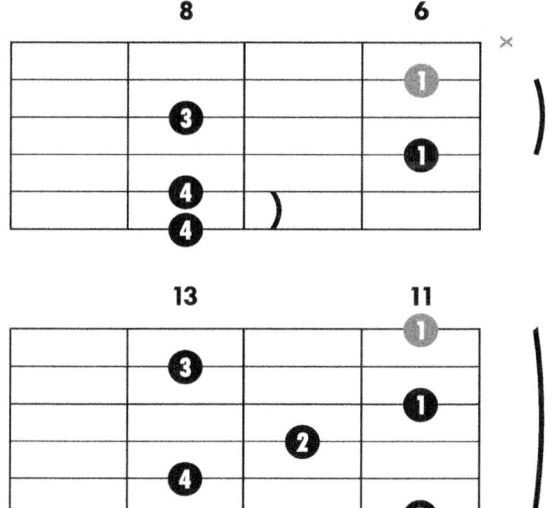

E♭m13

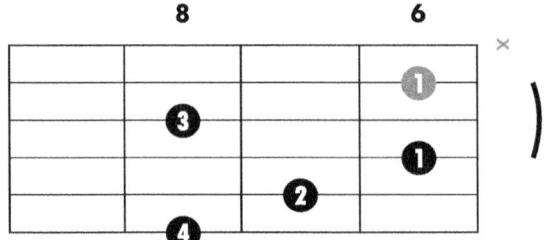

E♭add9

E♭sus4

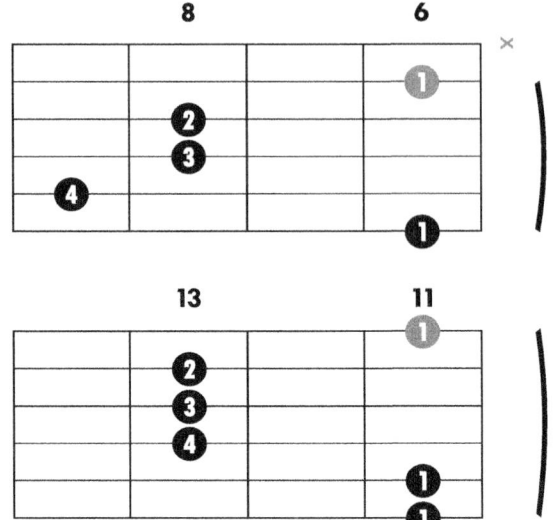

E♭7sus4

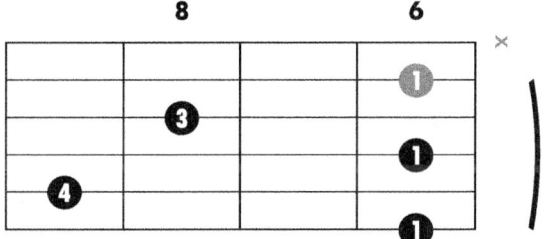

E♭6/9

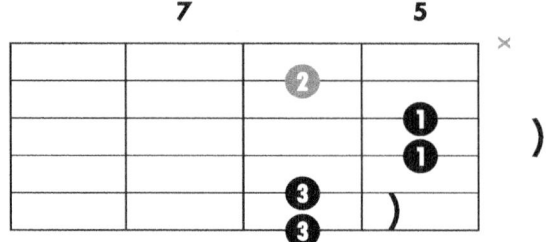

E♭aug

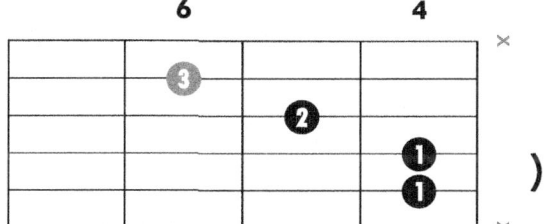

E♭7#9

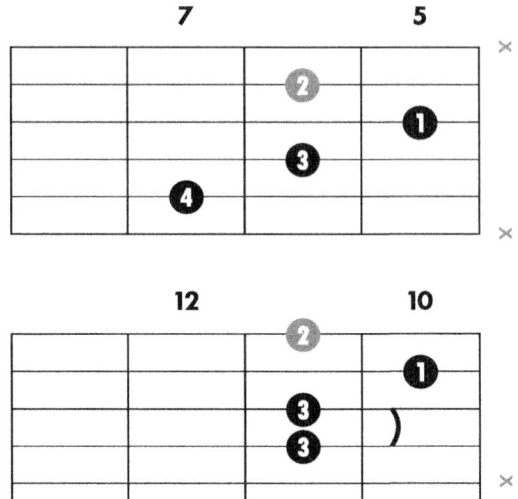

E

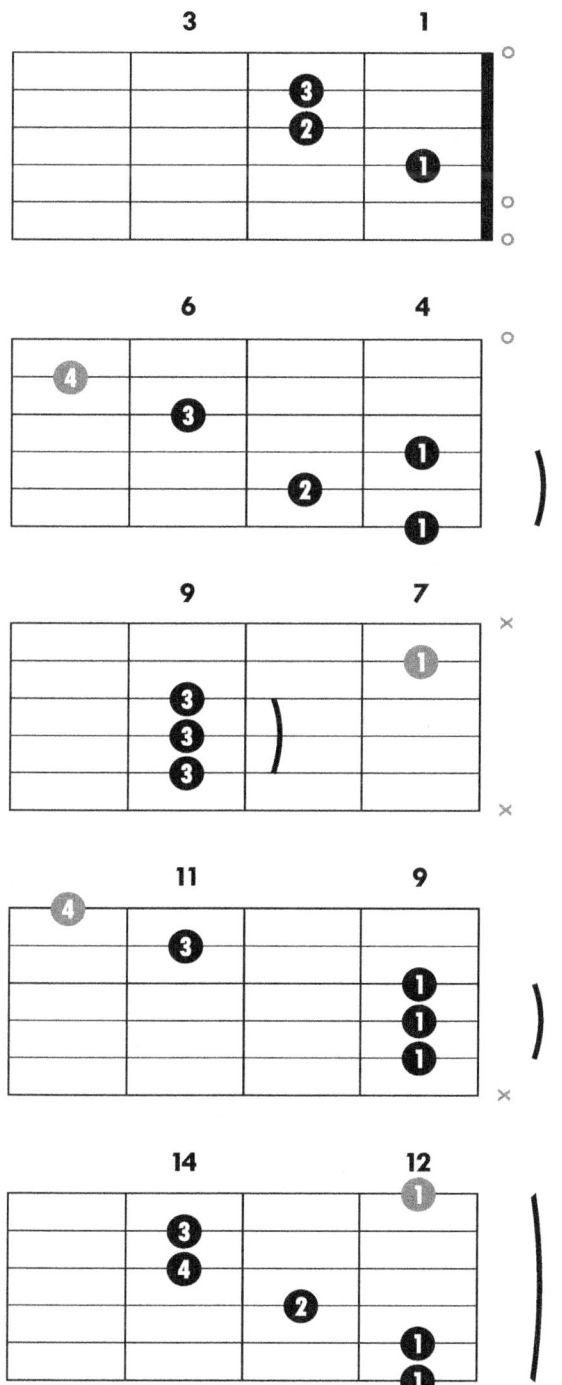

Em

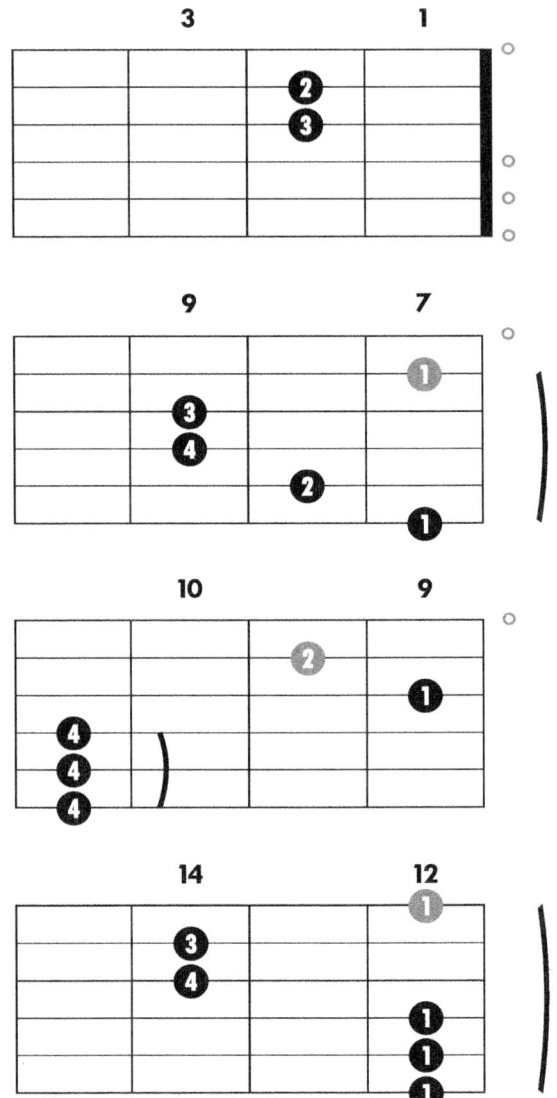

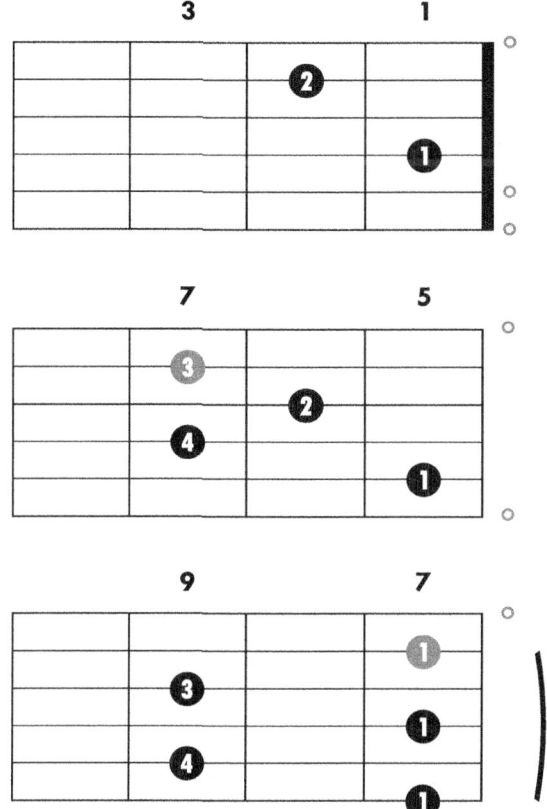

Em7

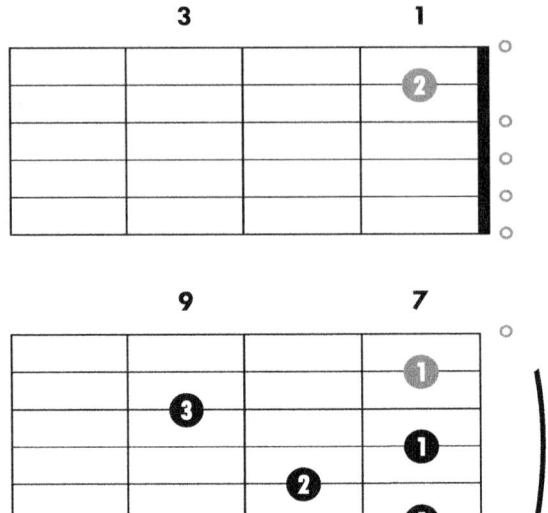

Emaj7

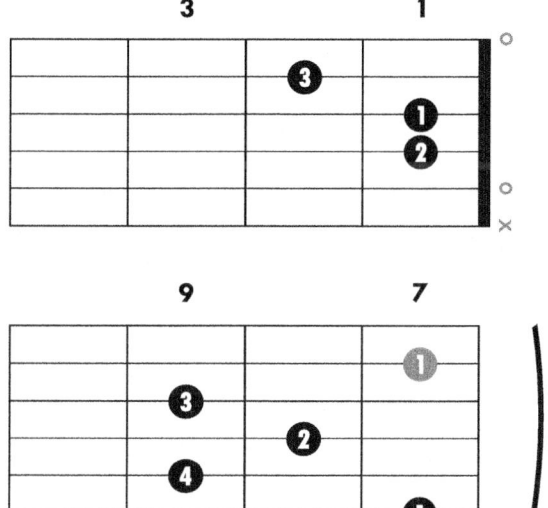

E5

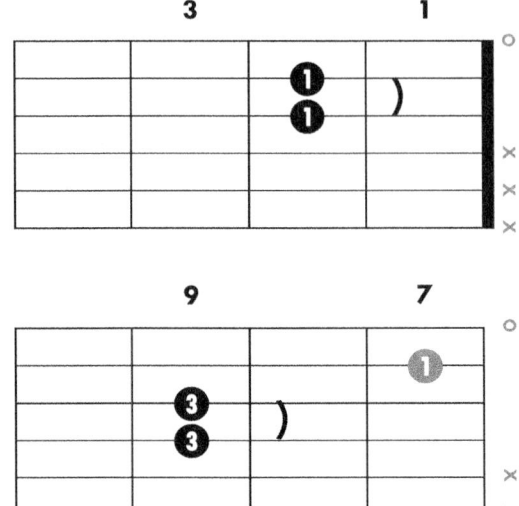

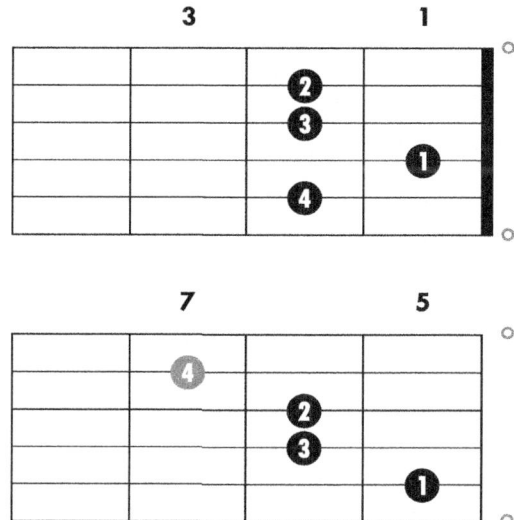

Em6

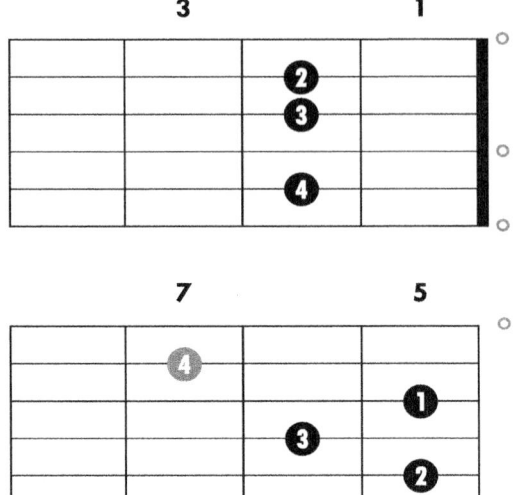

E9

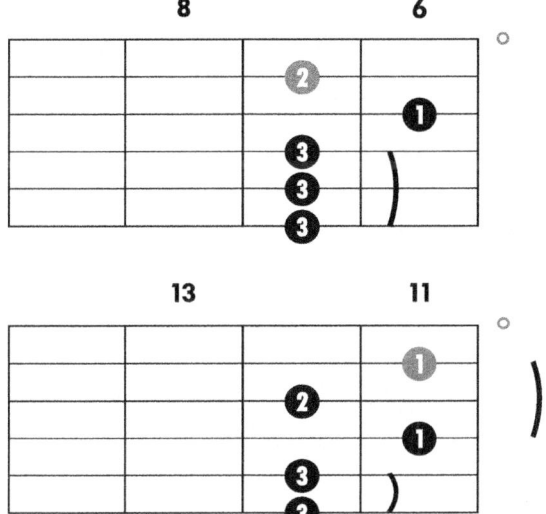

Em9

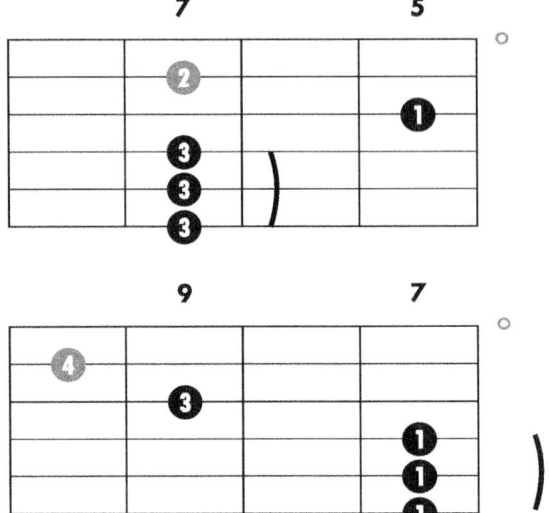

Emaj9

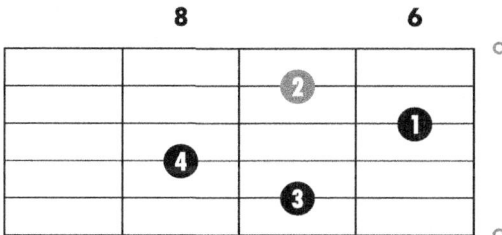

Edim7

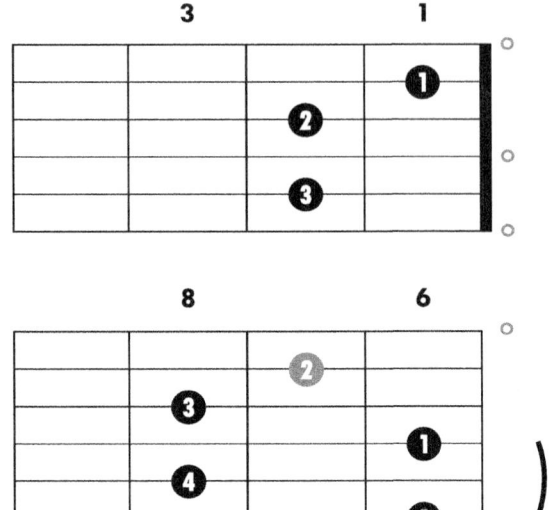

E11

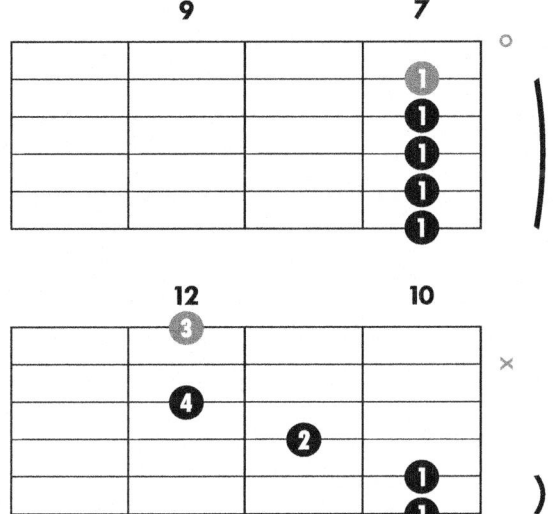

E13

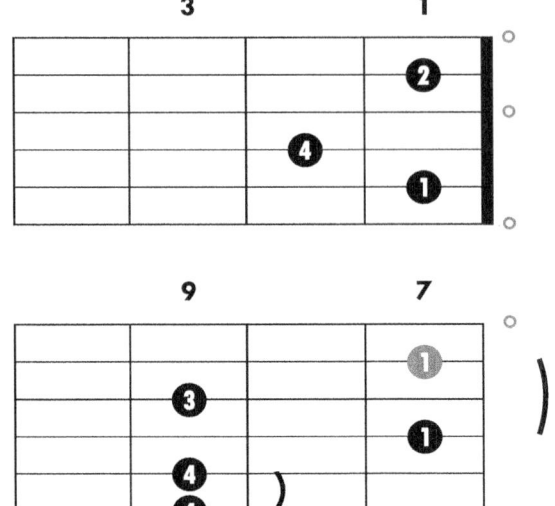

Em13

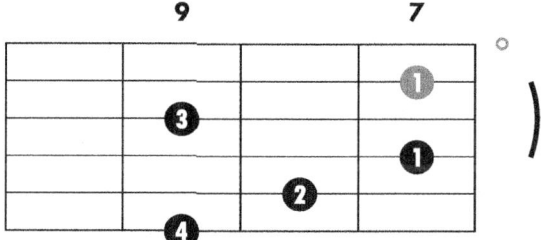

Eadd9

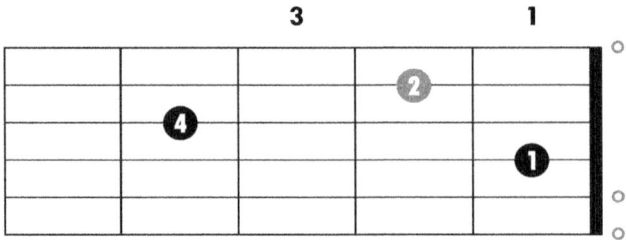

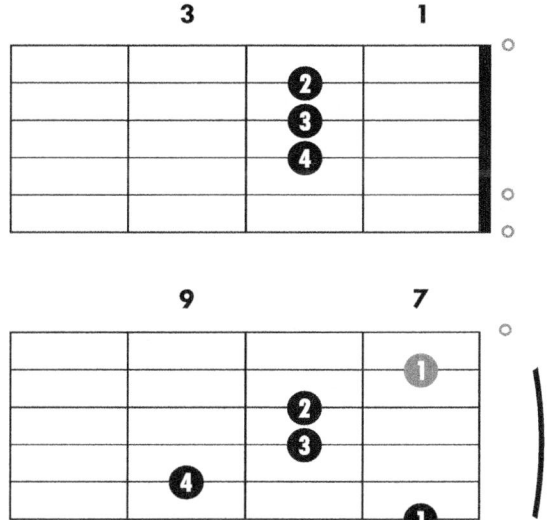

E7sus4

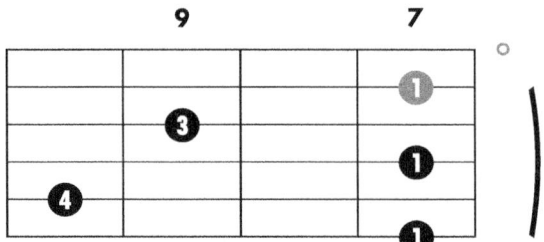

E6/9

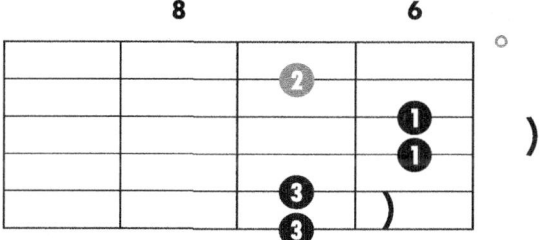

Eaug

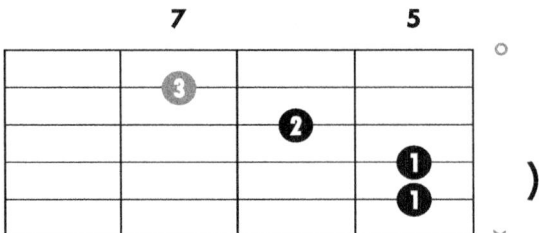

E7#9

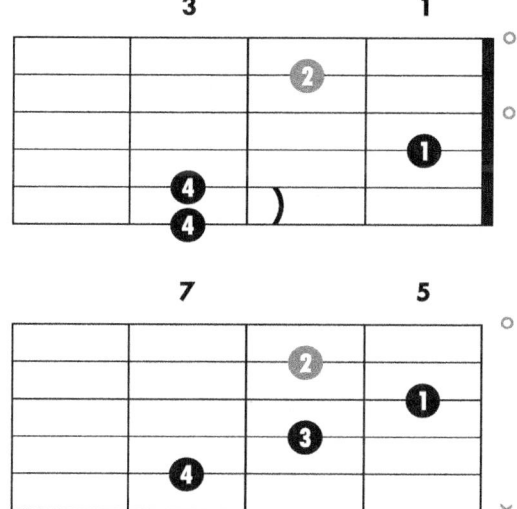

F

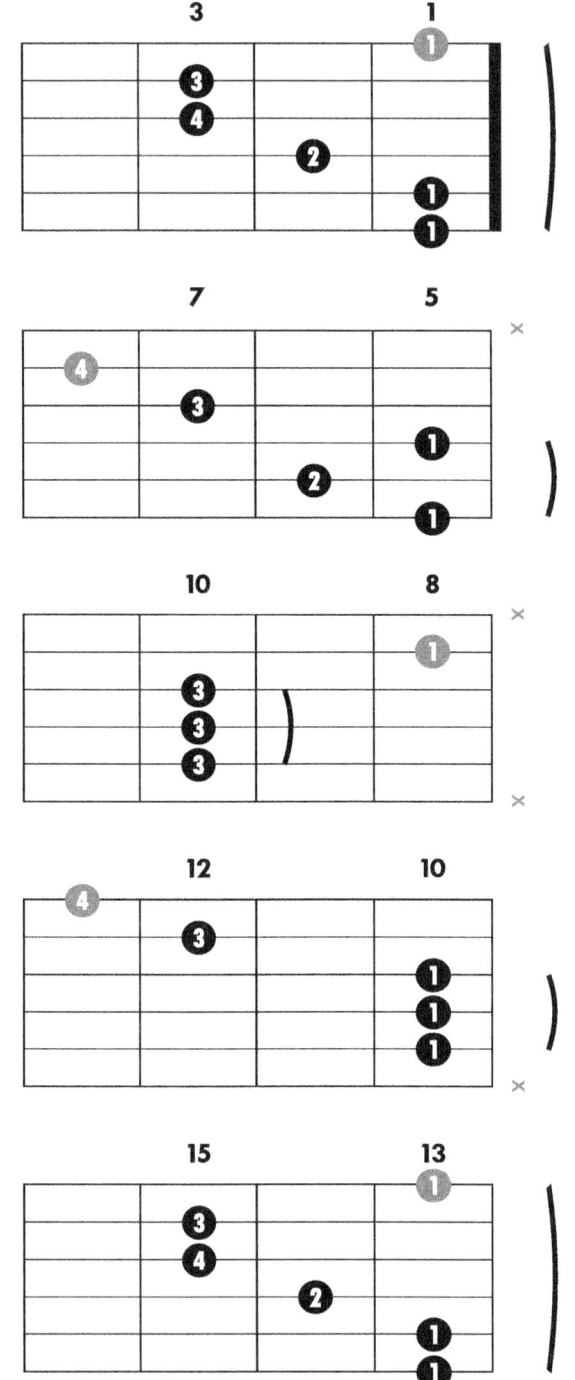

Fm

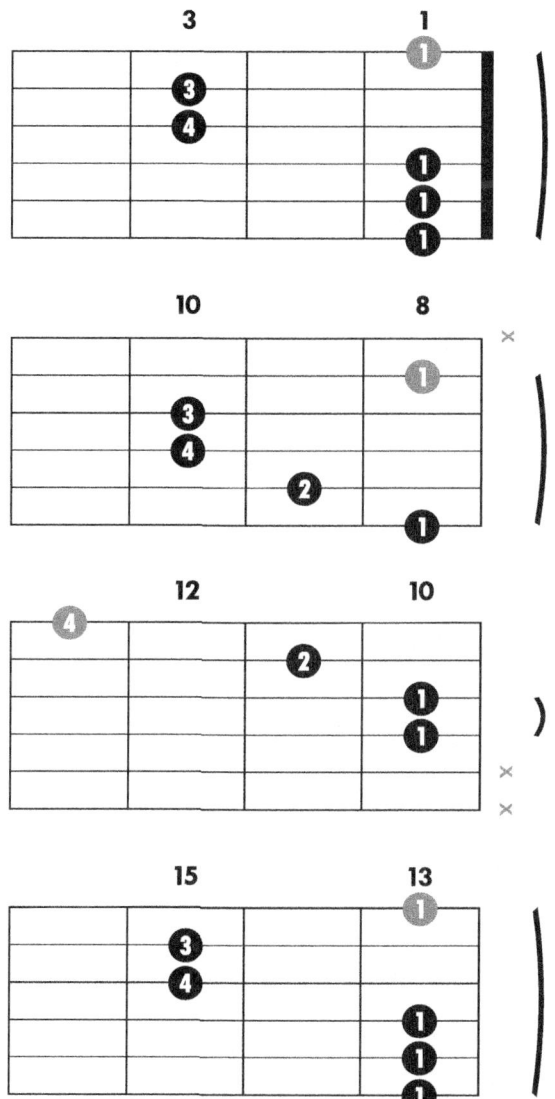

F7

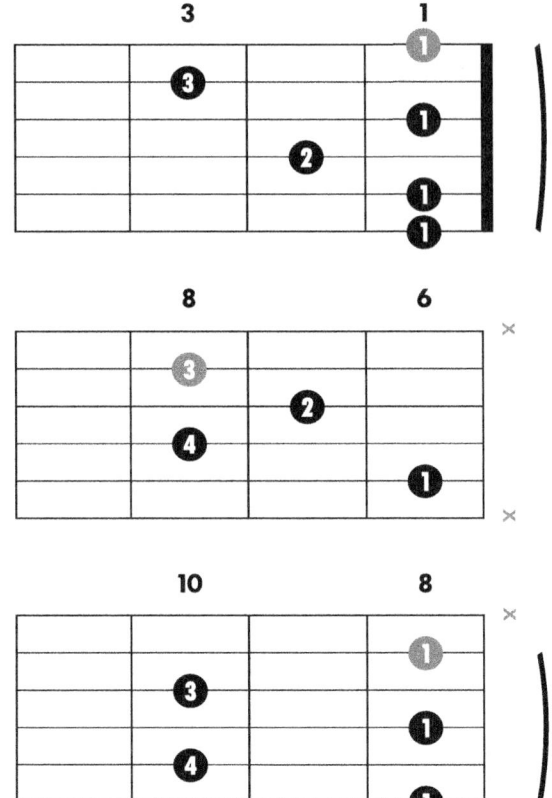

Fm7

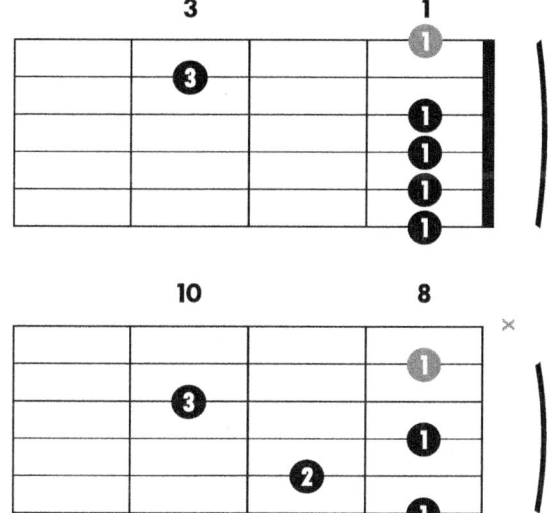

Fmaj7

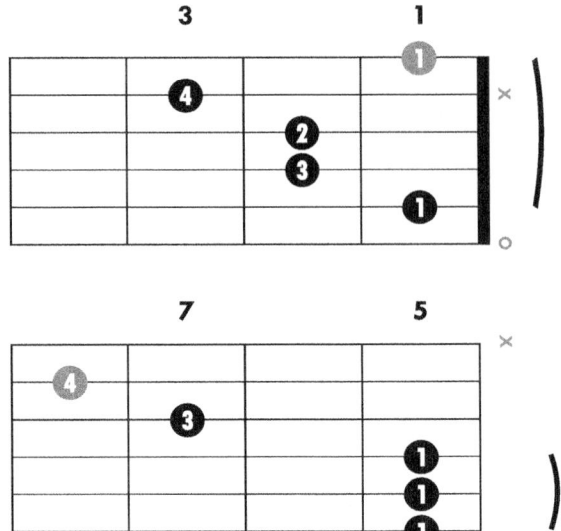

F5

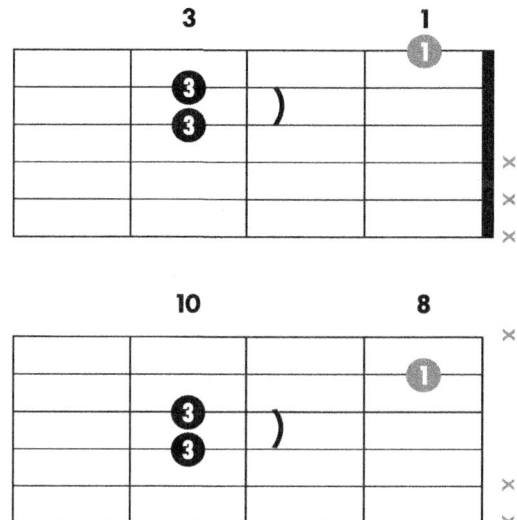

F6

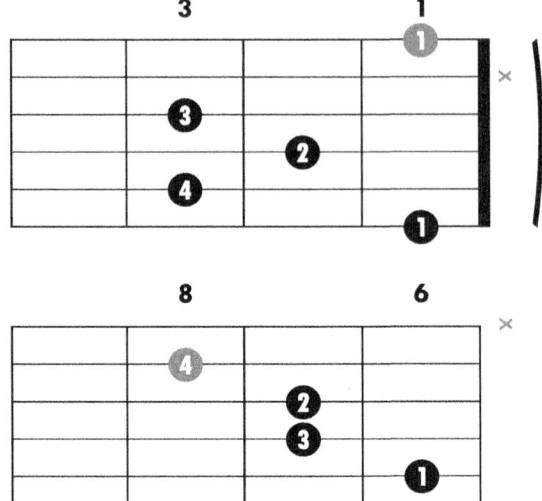

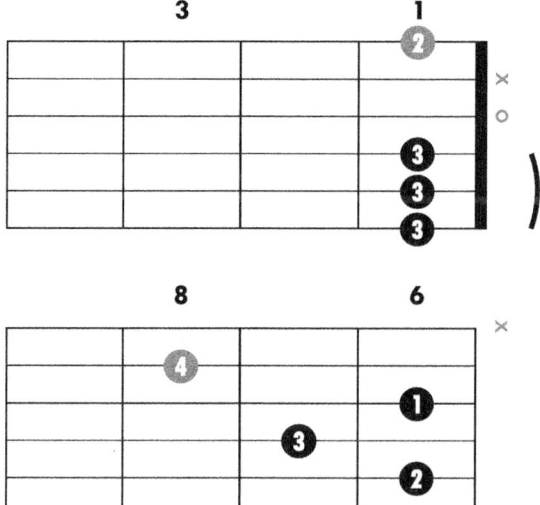

F9

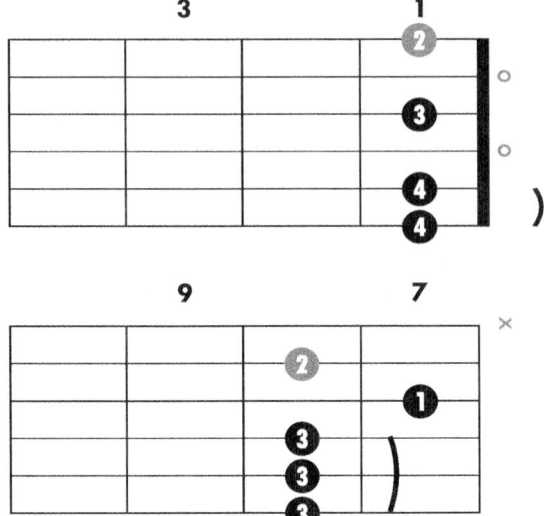

Fm9

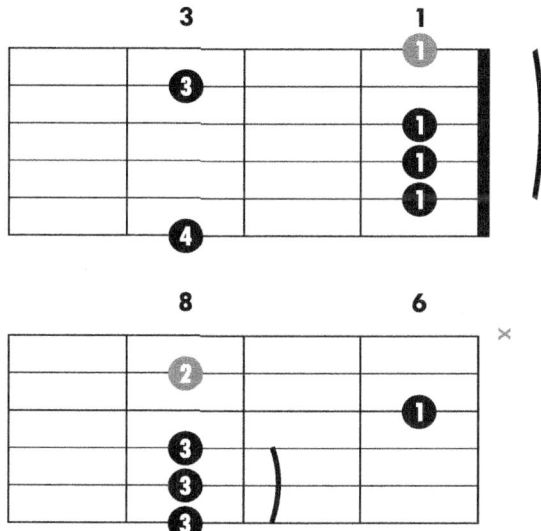

Fmaj9

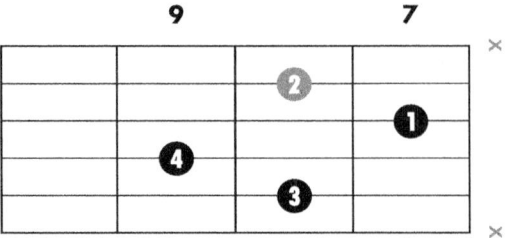

Fdim7

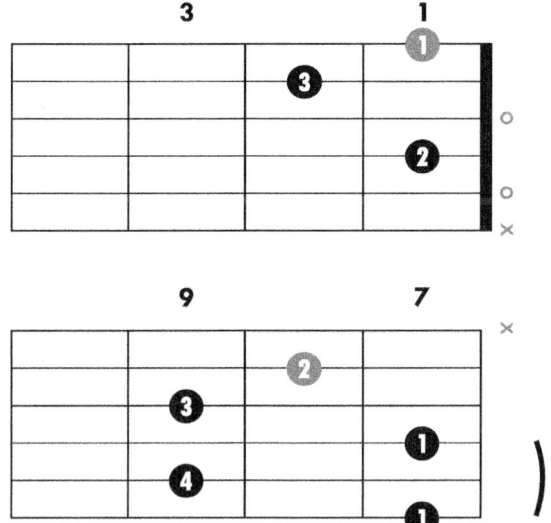

F11

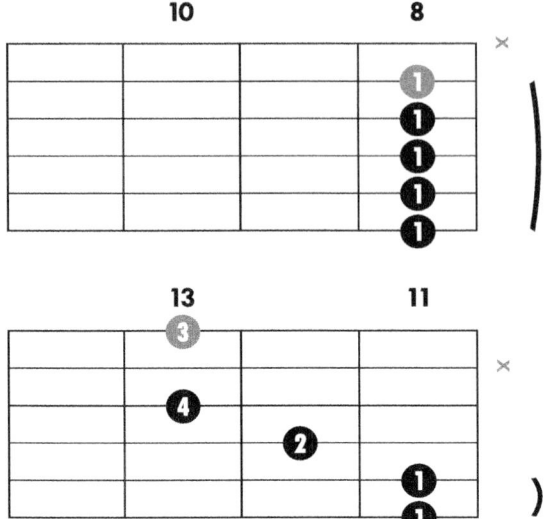

F13

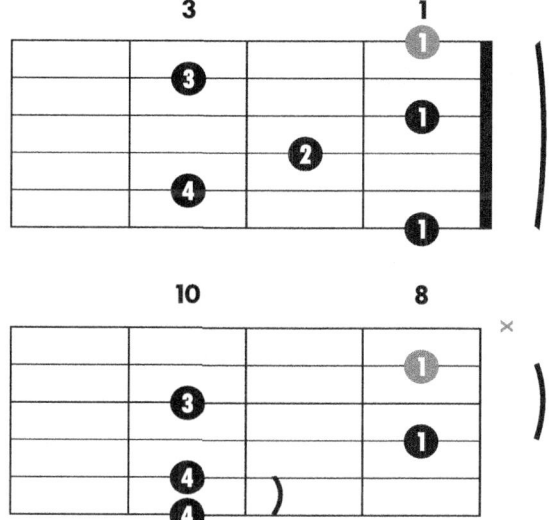

Fm13

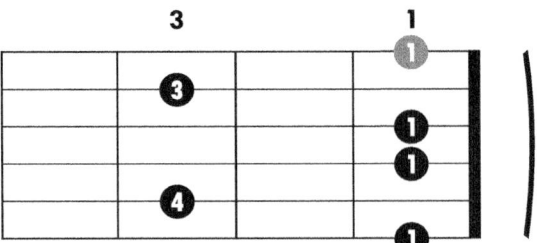

Fadd9

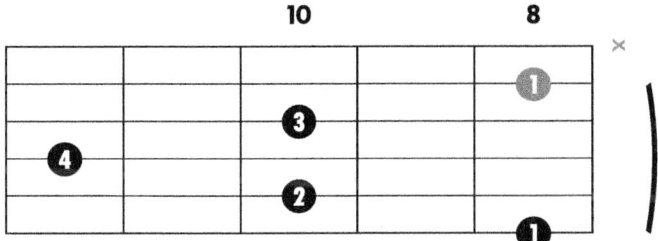

Fsus4

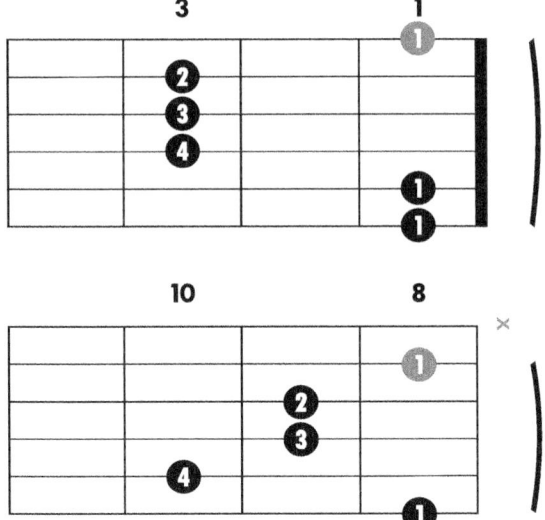

F7sus4

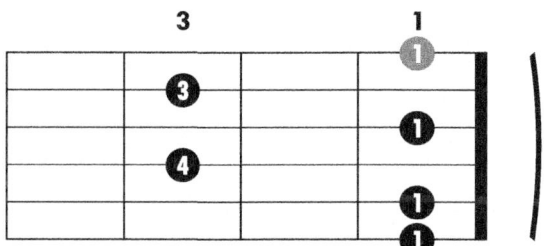

F6/9

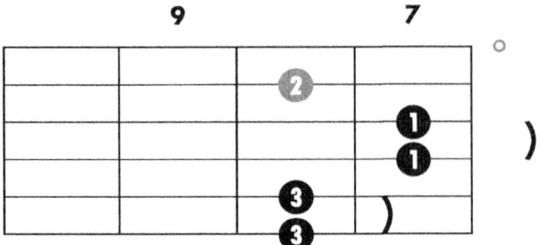

Faug

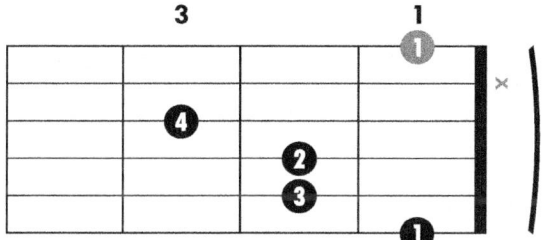

F7#9

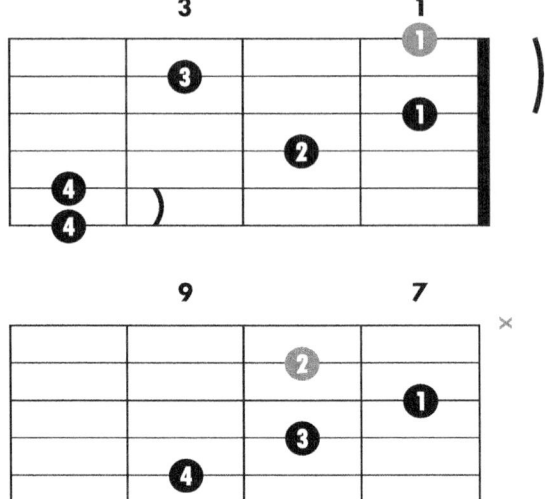

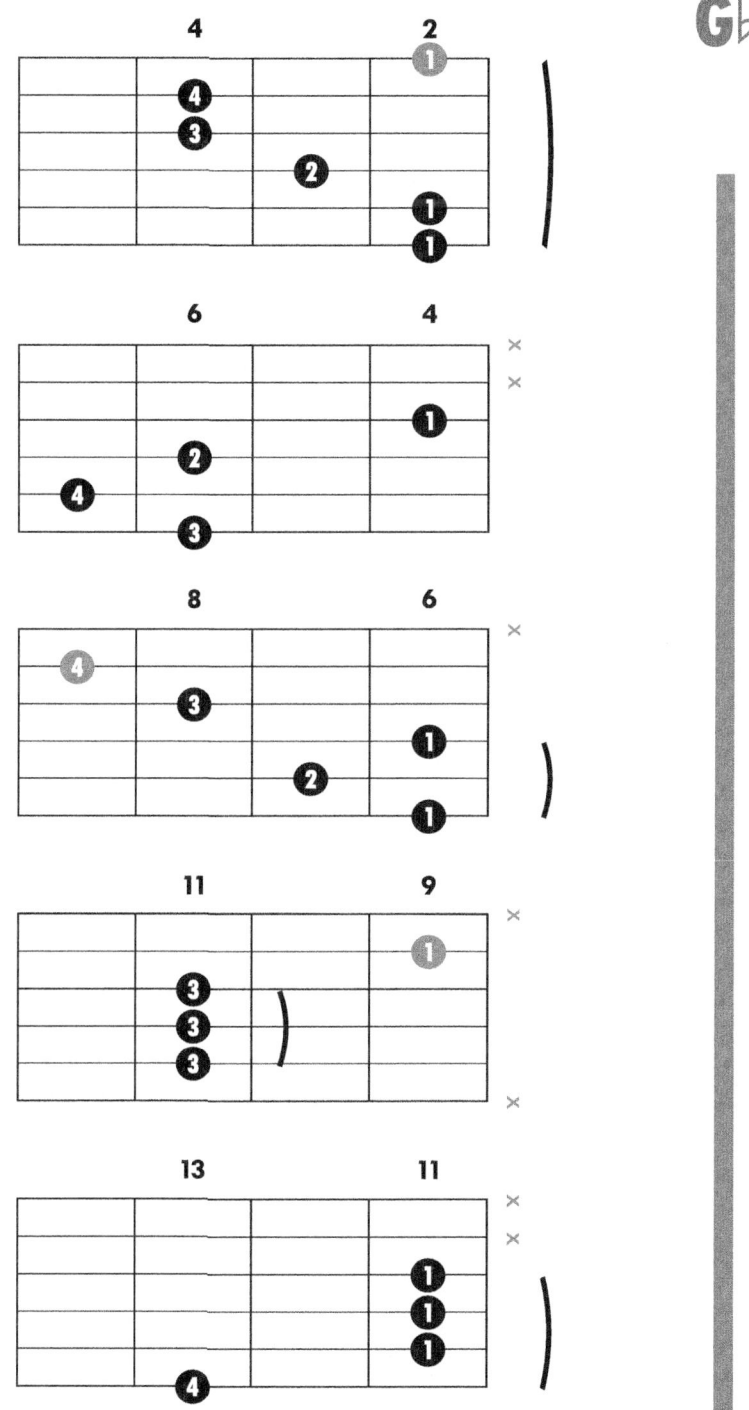

F#
Gb

F#m

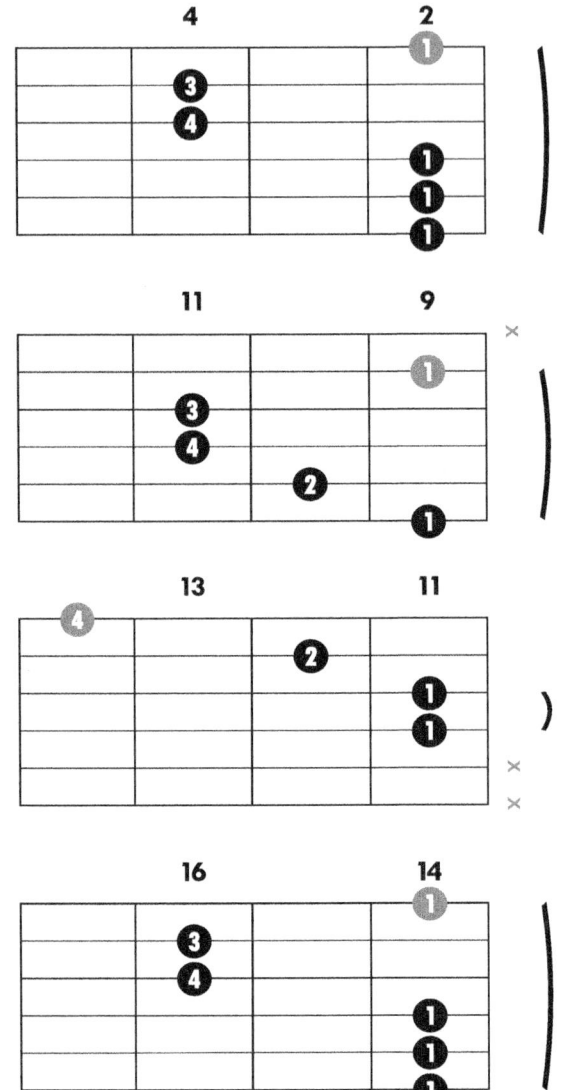

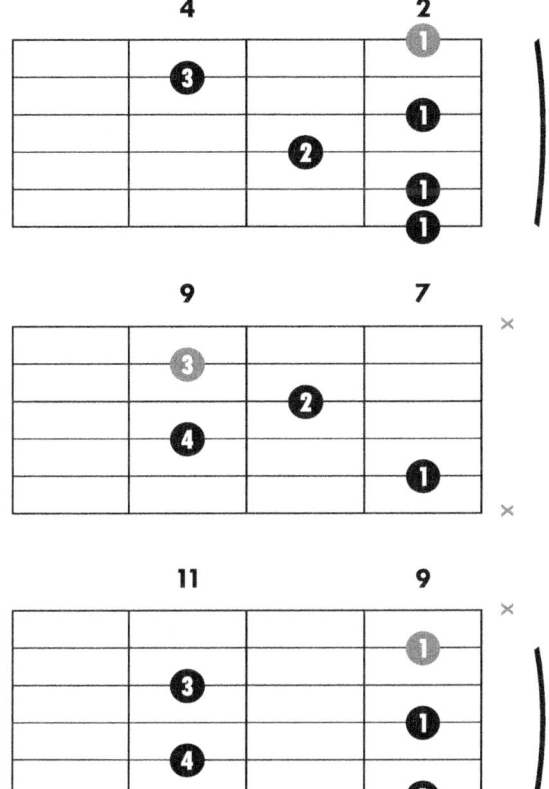

F#m7

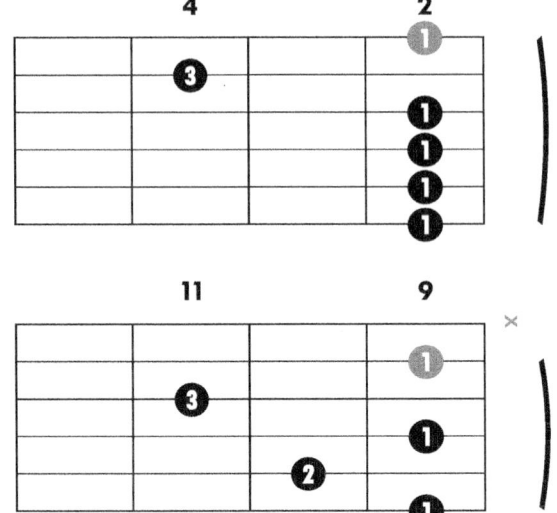

F#maj7

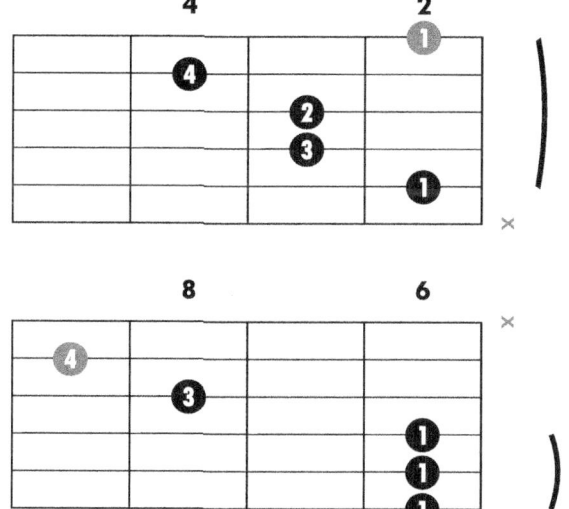

F#5

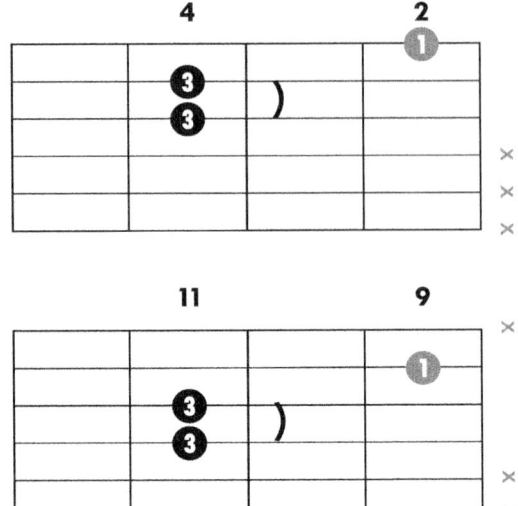

F#6

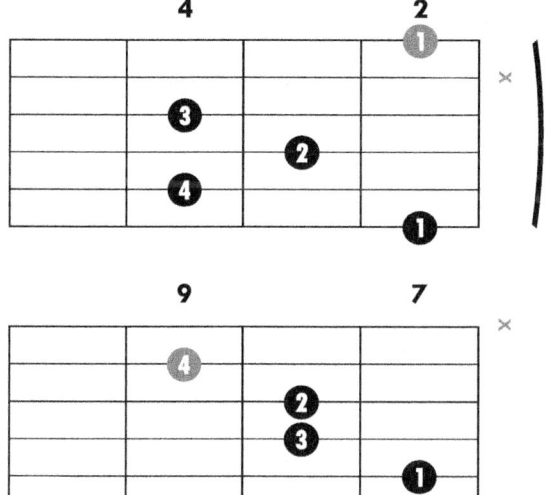

F#m6

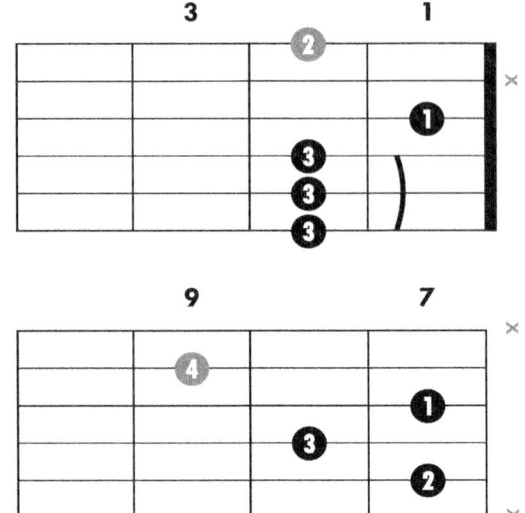

F#9

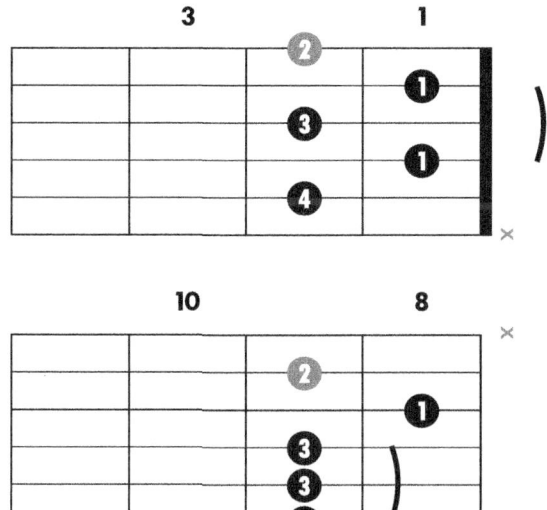

F#m9

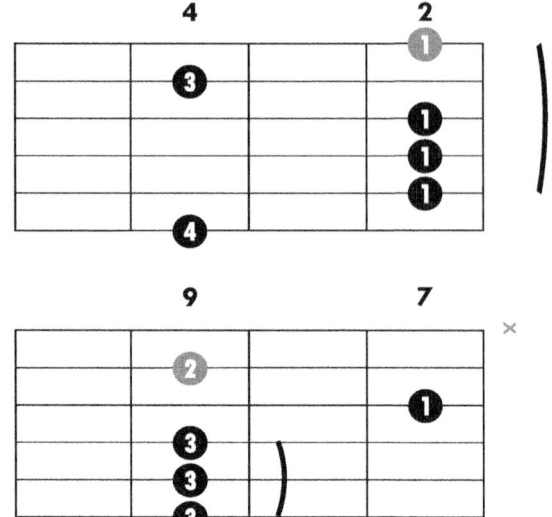

F#maj9

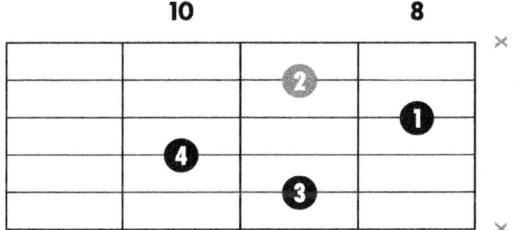

F#dim7

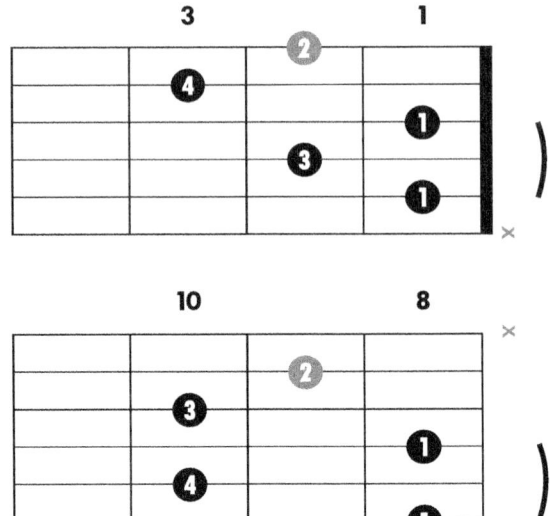

F#11

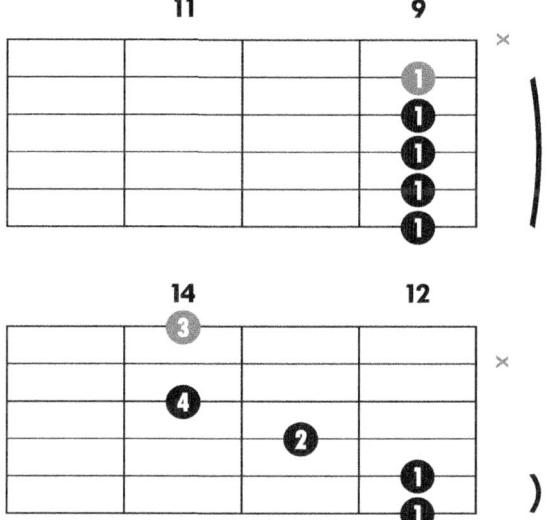

F#13

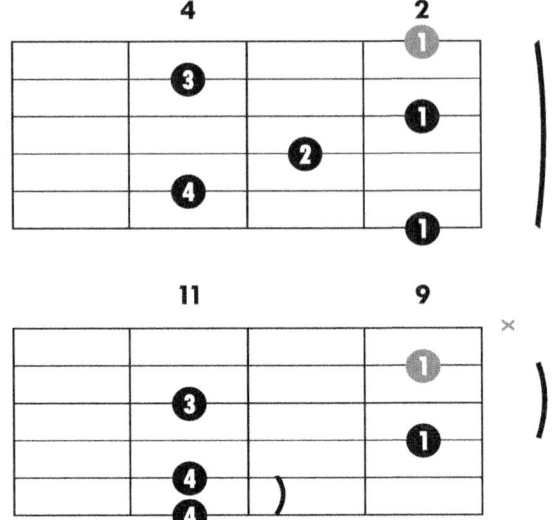

F#m13

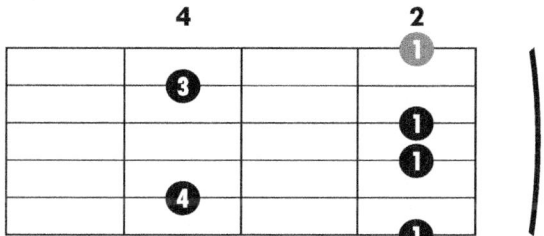

F#add9

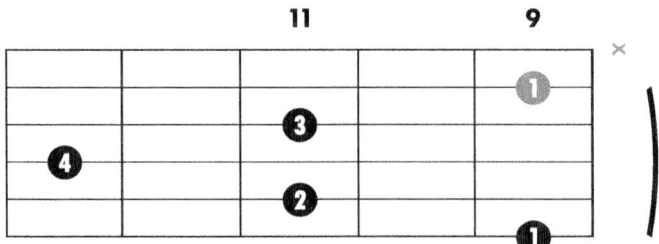

F#sus4

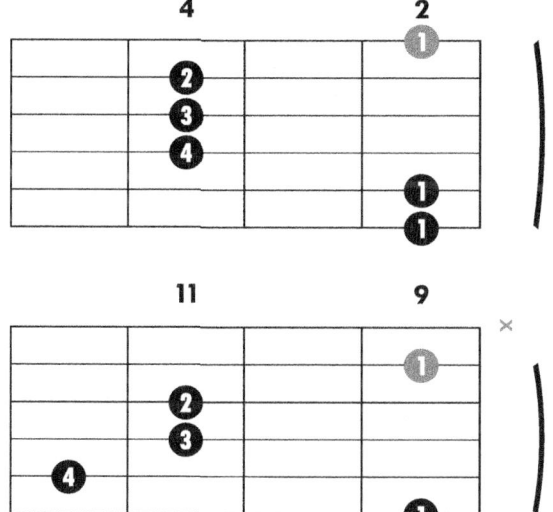

F#7sus4

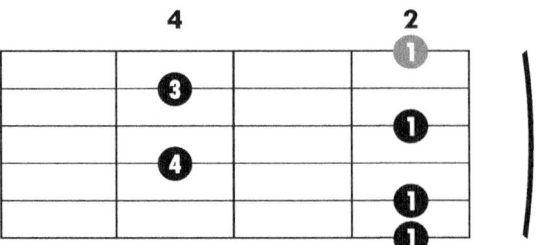

F#6/9

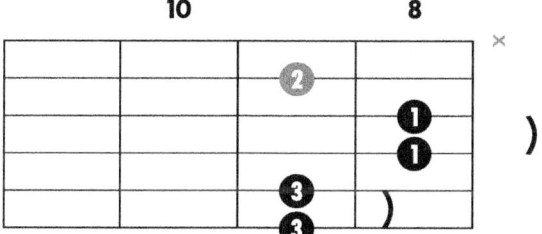

F#aug

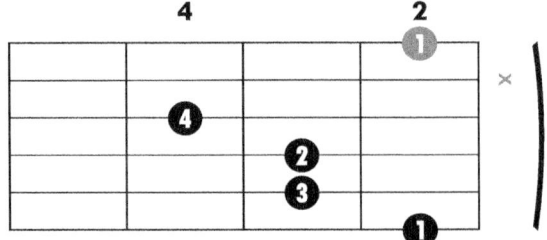

F#7#9

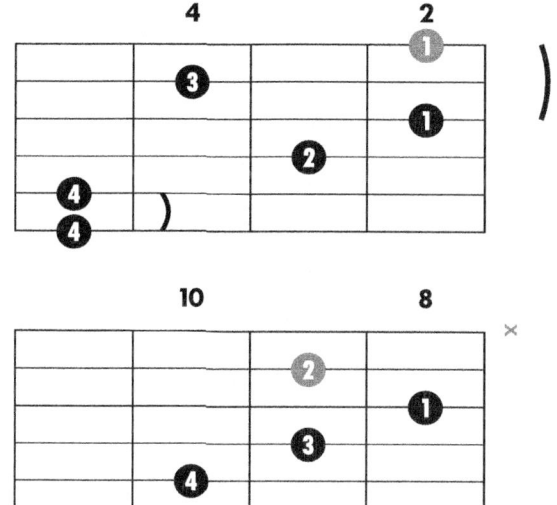

G

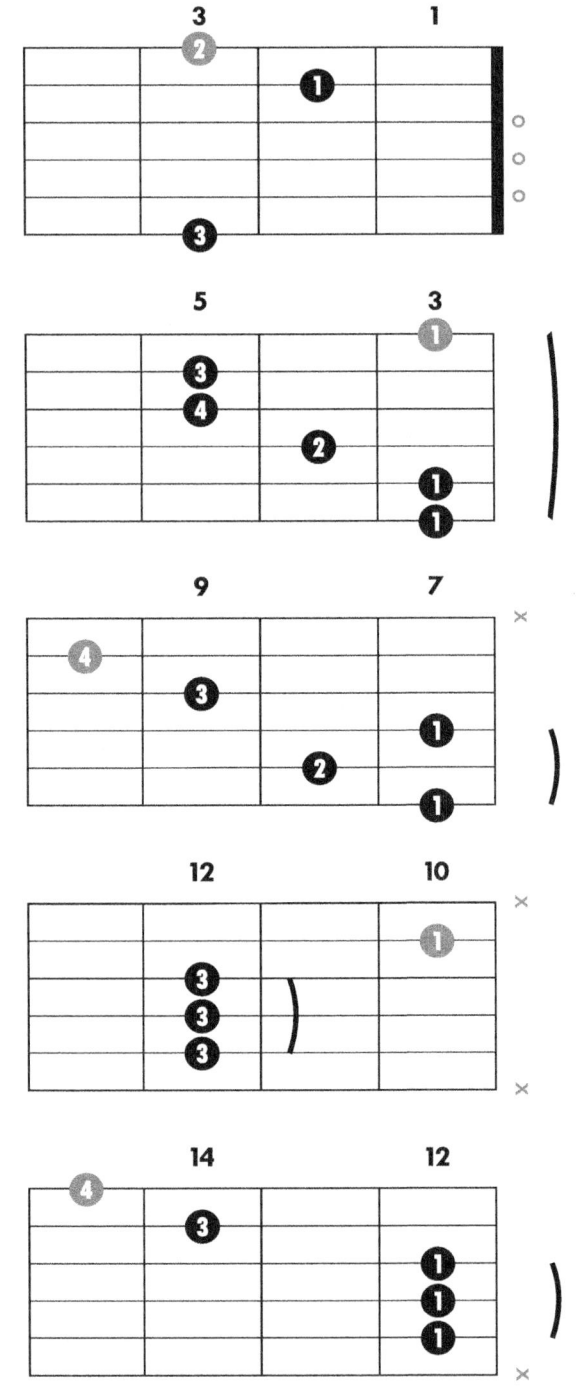

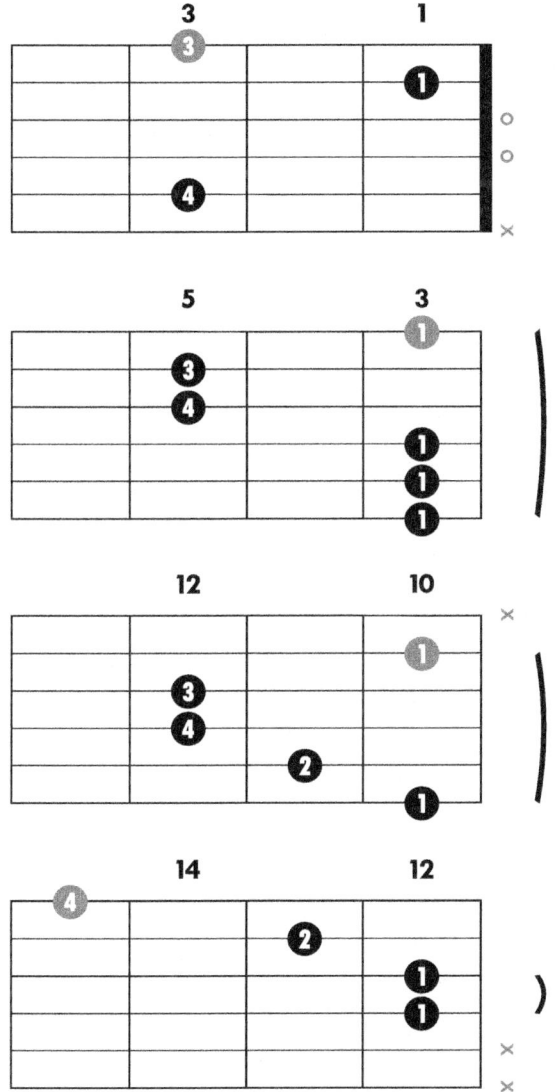

G7

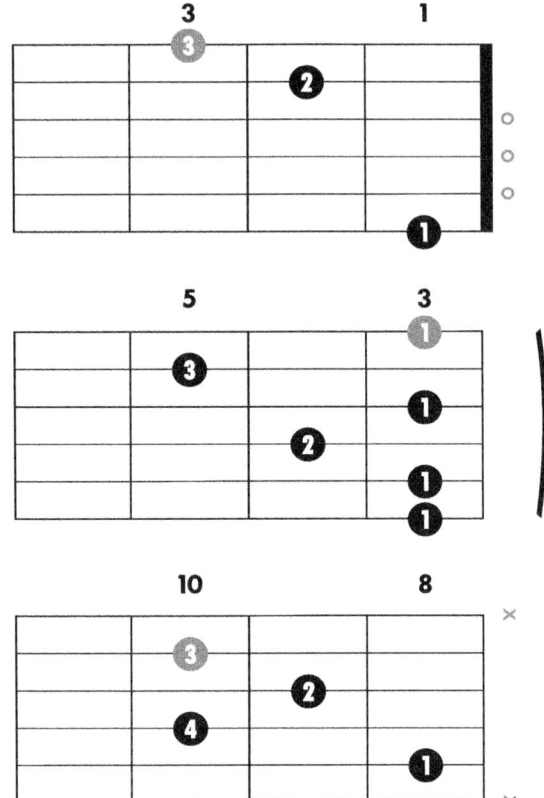

Gm7

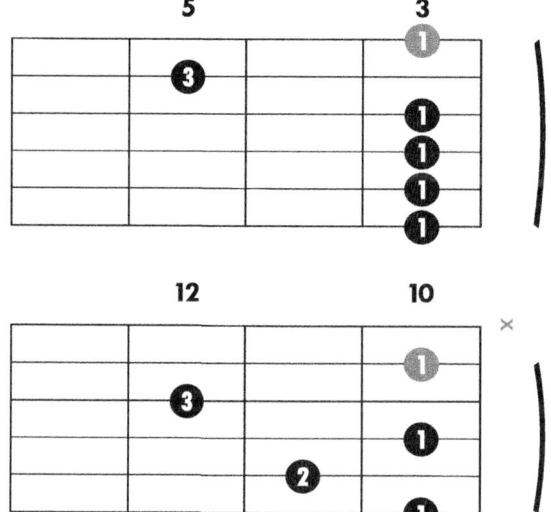

Gmaj7

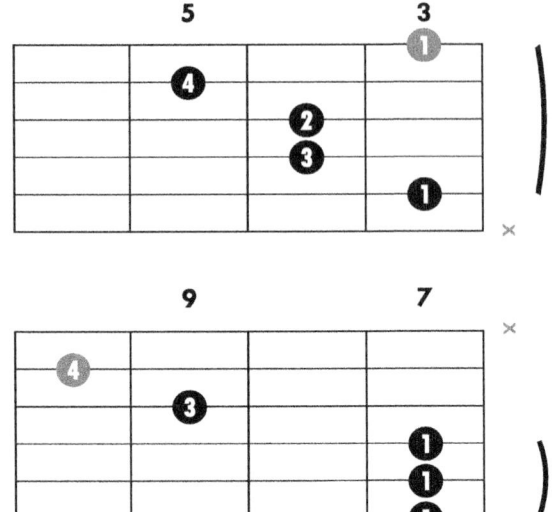

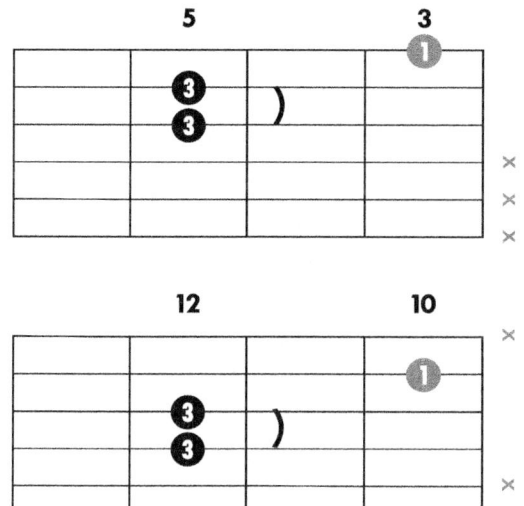

G6

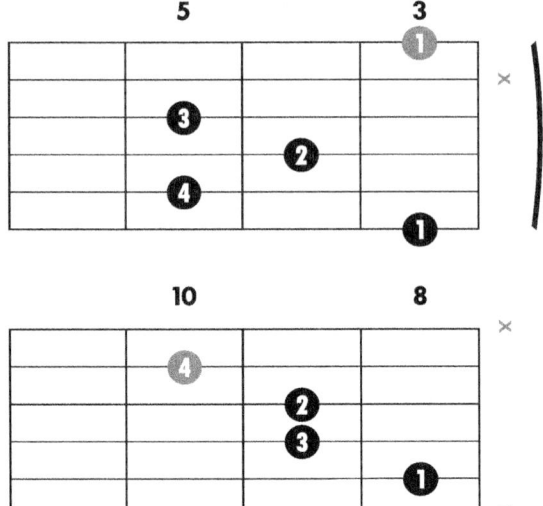

Gm6

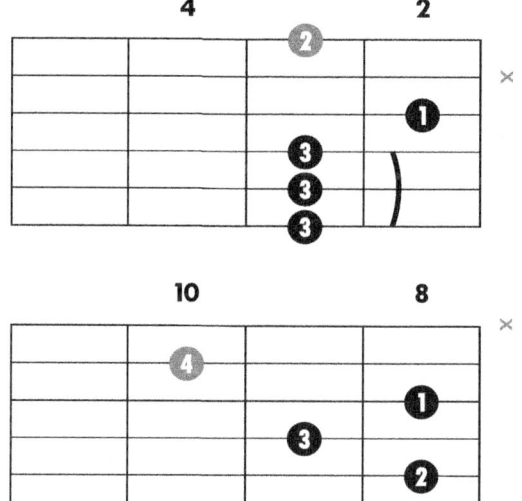

G9

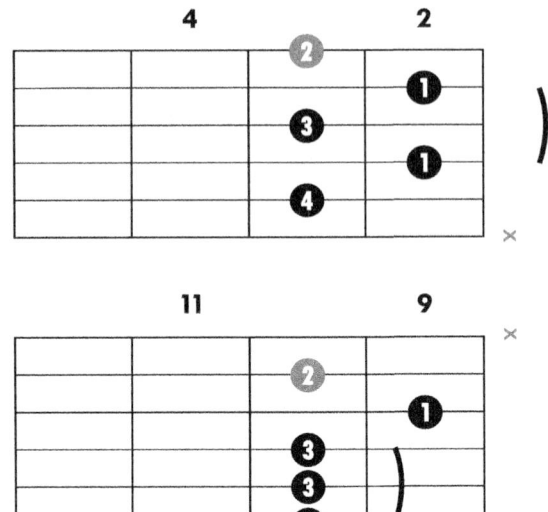

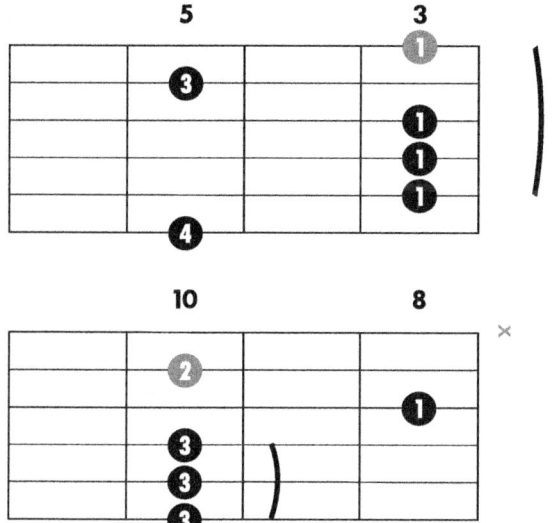

Gmaj9

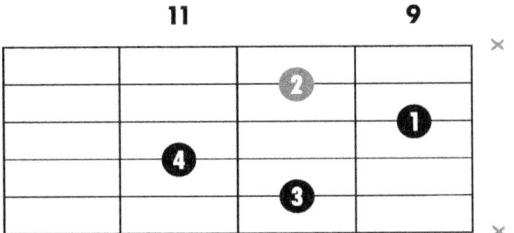

Gdim7

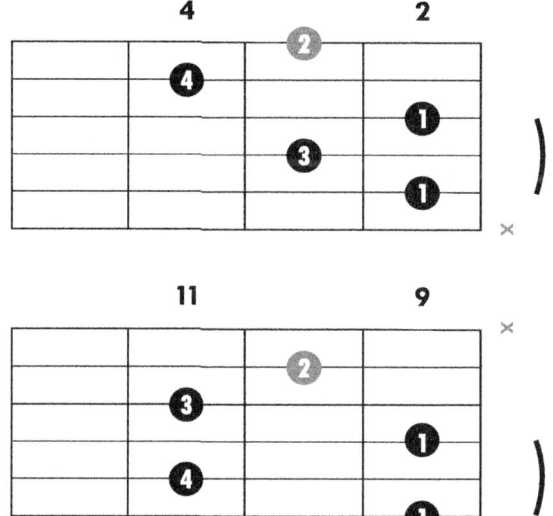

G11

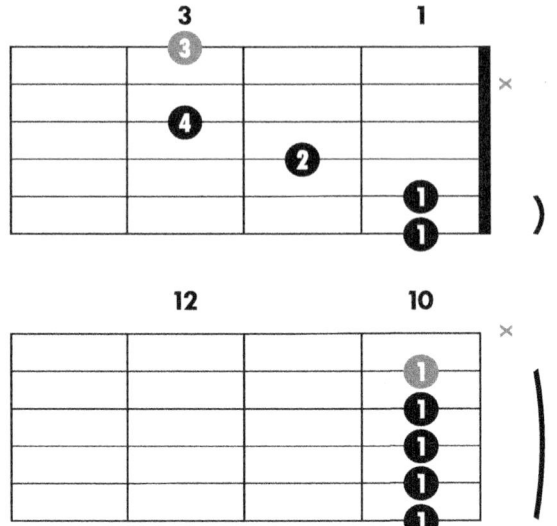

G13

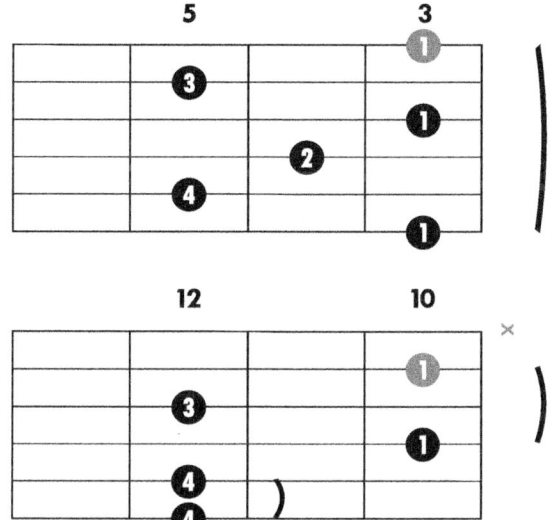

Gm13

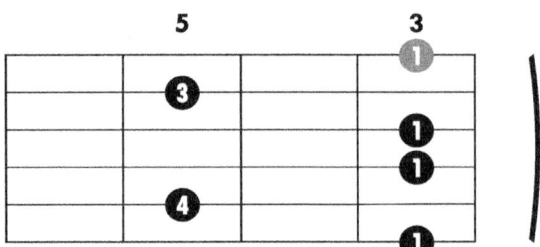

Gadd9

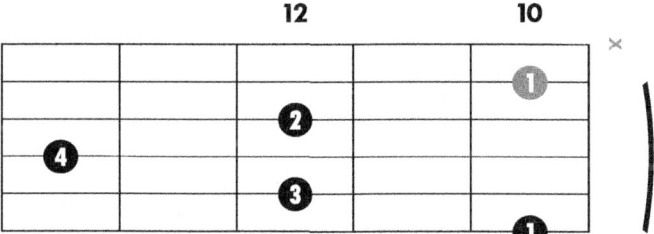

Gsus4

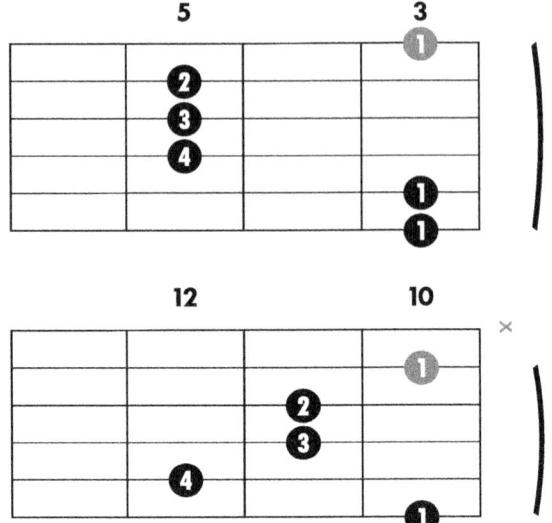

G7sus4

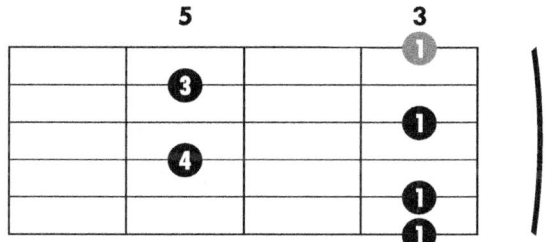

G6/9

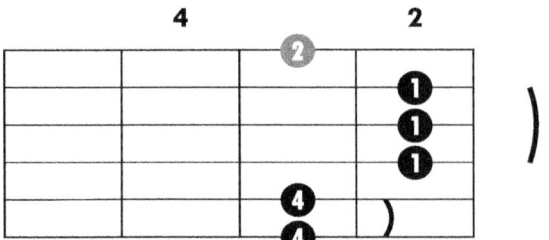

Gaug

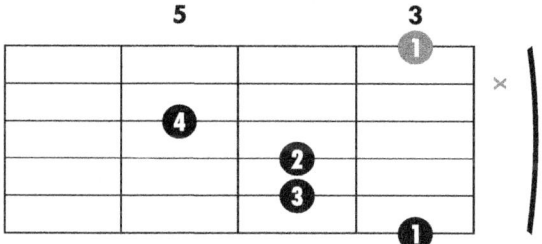

G7#9

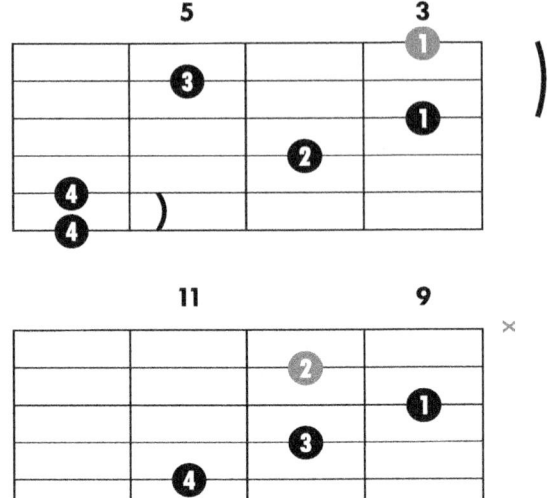

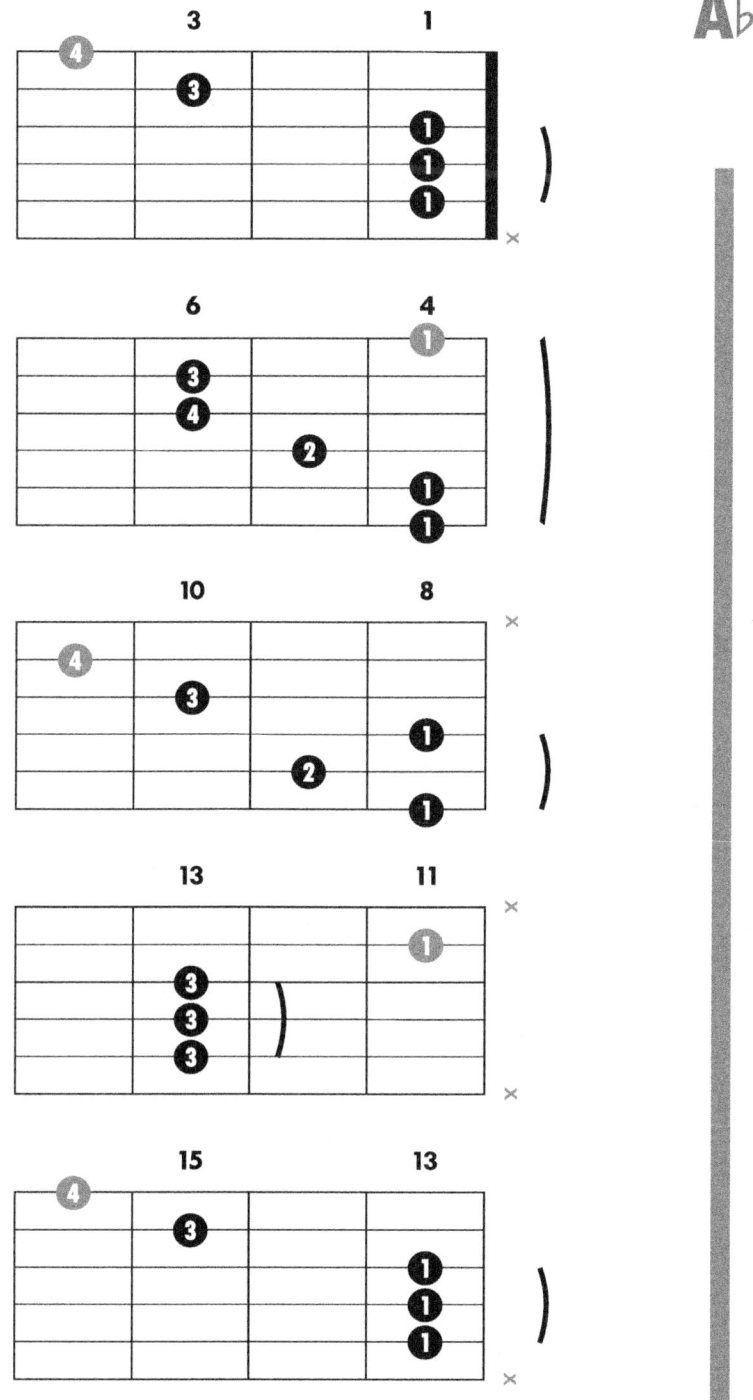

G#
Ab

A♭m

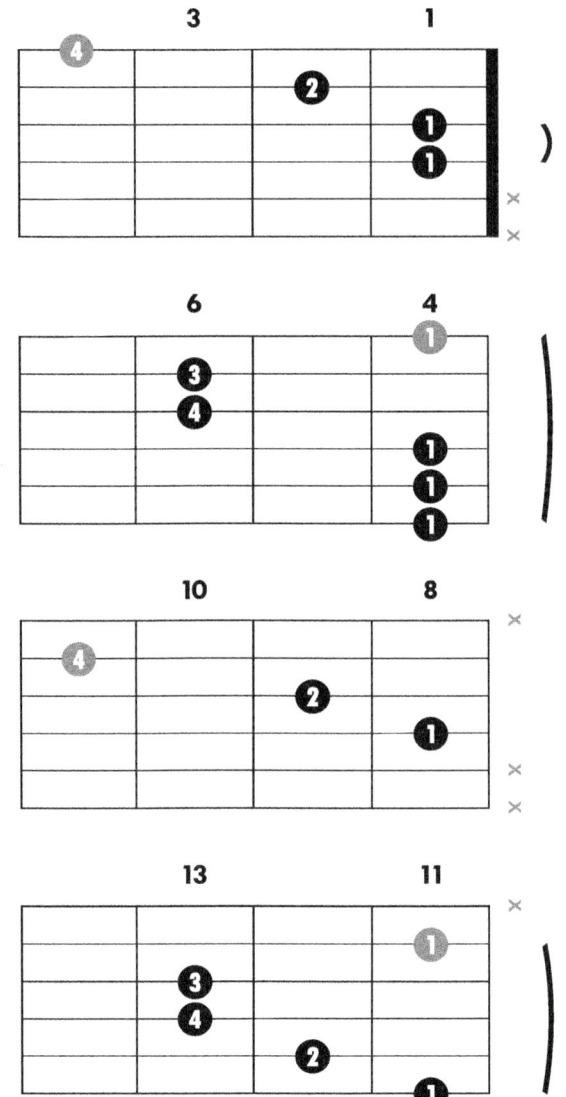

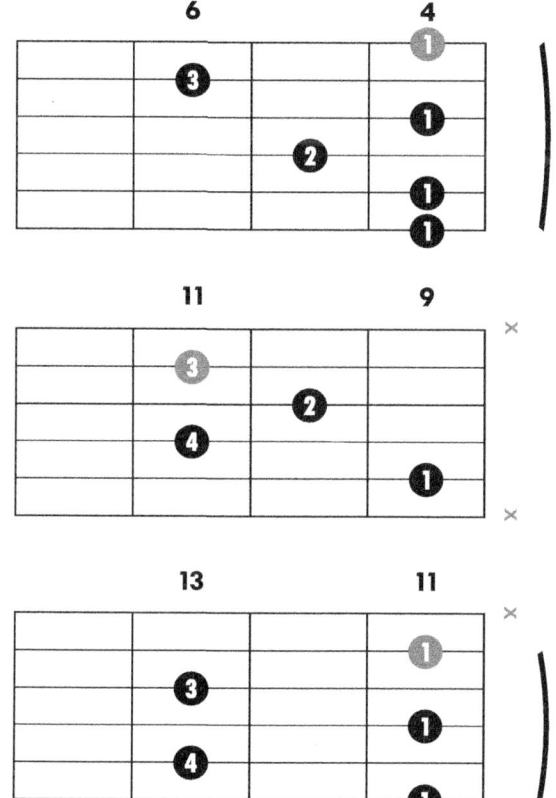

A♭m7

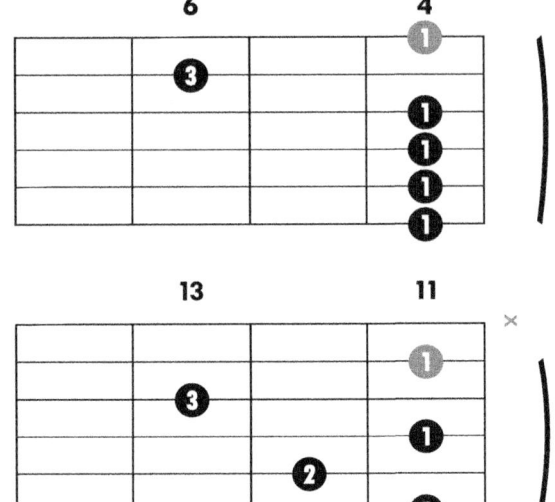

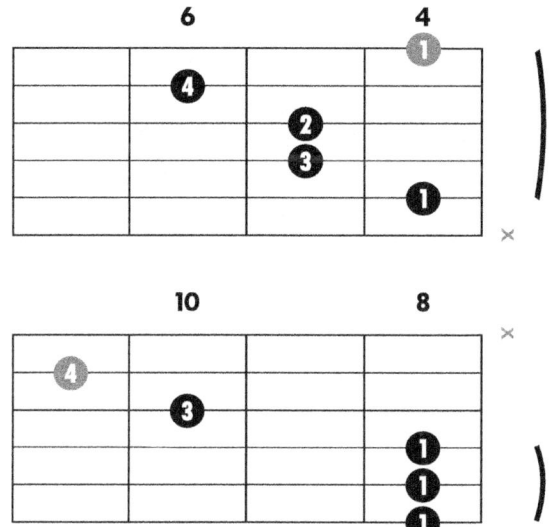

A♭5

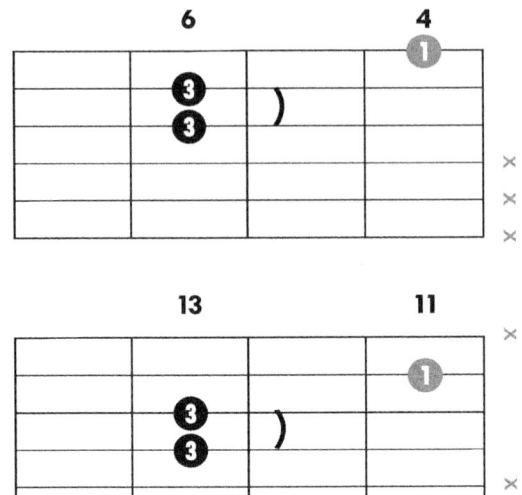

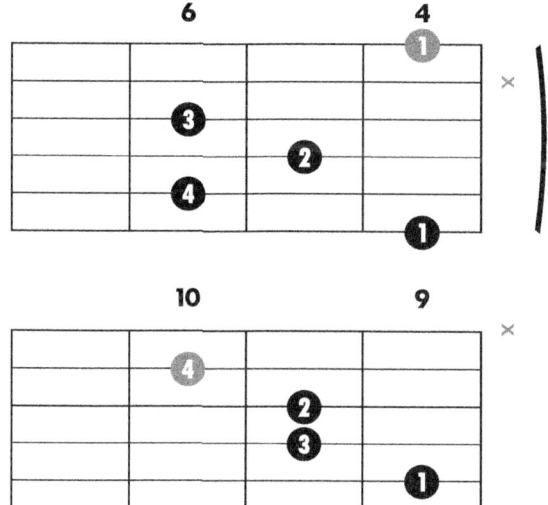

A♭m6

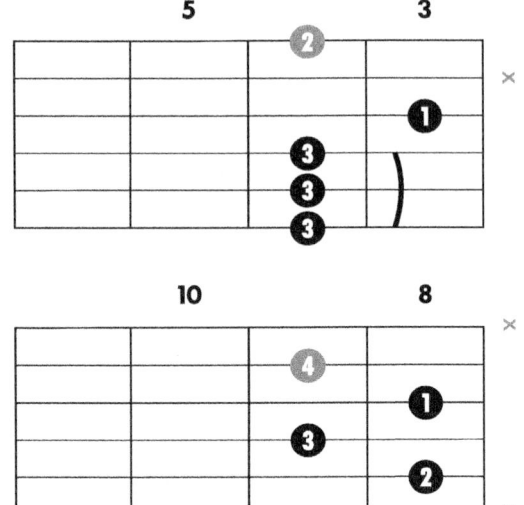

A♭9

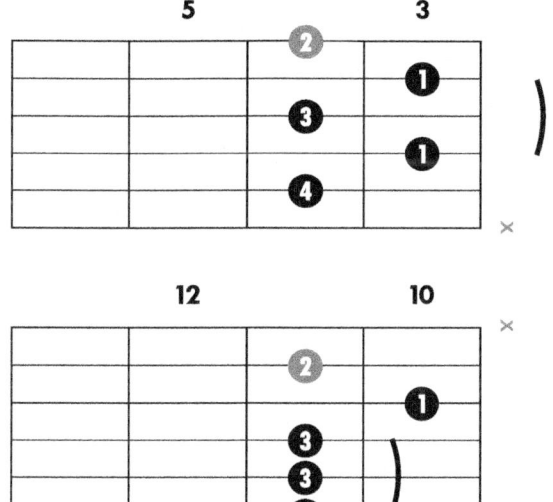

A♭m9

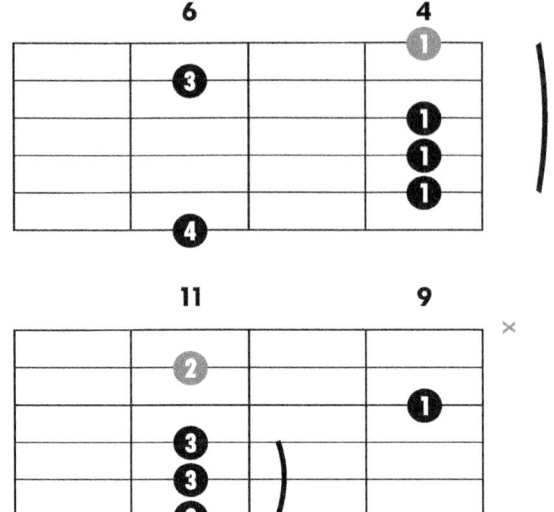

A♭maj9

A♭dim7

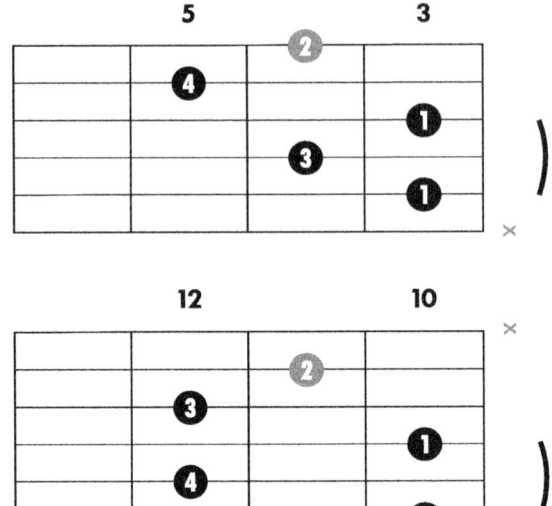

A♭11

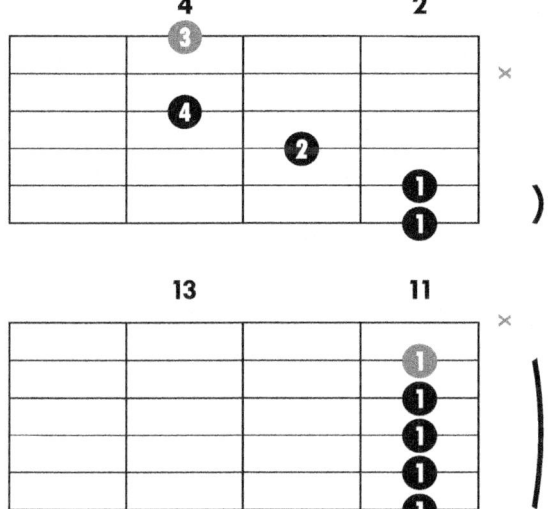

A♭13

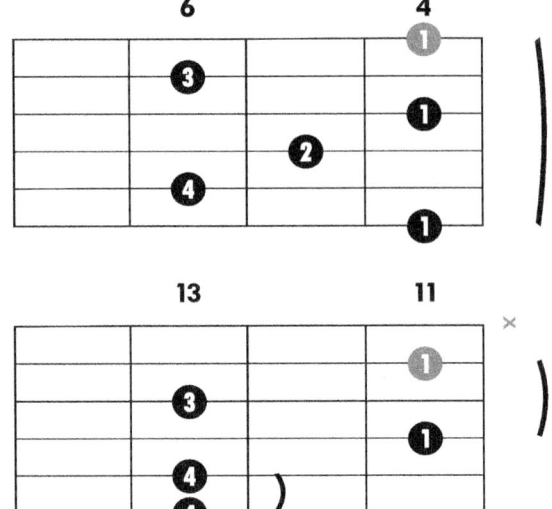

A♭m13

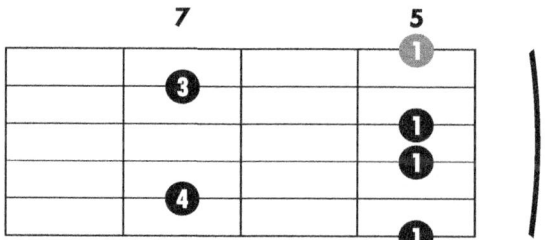

A♭add9

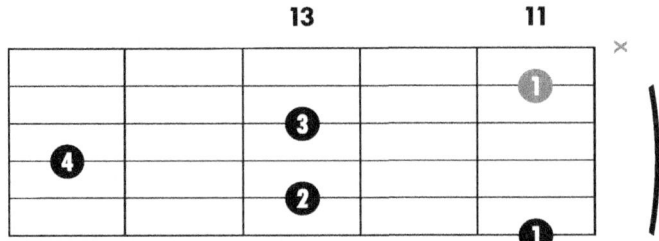

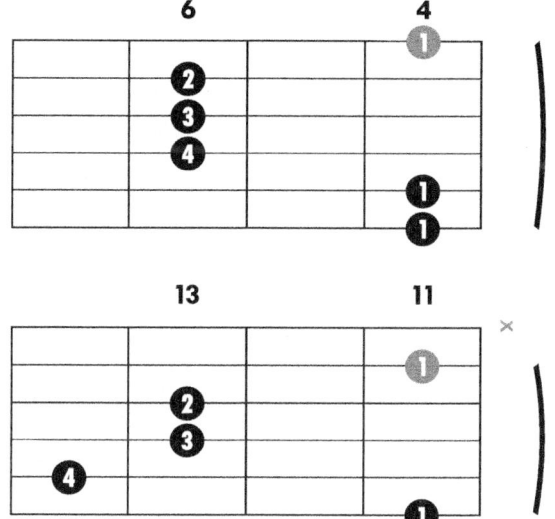

A♭7sus4

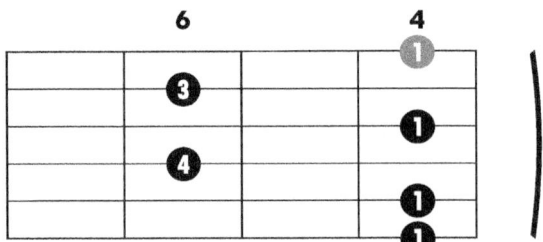

A♭6/9

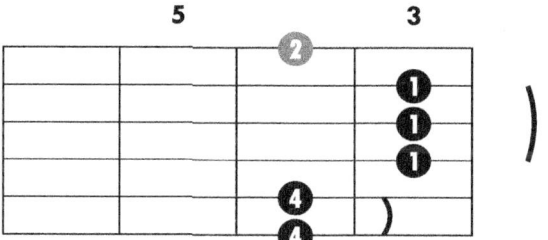

A♭aug

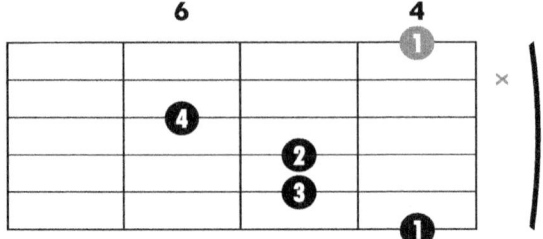

Ab7#9

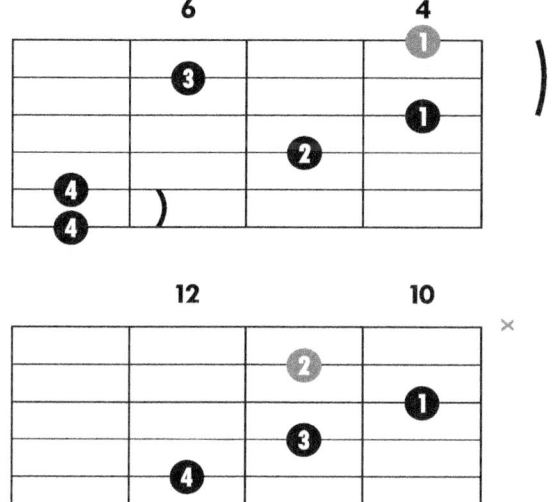

Terminology

M/maj	-	Major
m	-	Minor
7	-	Dominant Seventh
m7	-	Minor Seventh
maj7	-	Major Seventh
5	-	Power chord
6	-	Major Sixth
m6	-	Minor Sixth
9	-	Dominant Ninth
m9	-	Minor Ninth
maj9	-	Minor Ninth
dim7	-	Diminished Seventh
11	-	Dominant Eleventh
13	-	Dominant Thirteenth
m13	-	Minor Thirteenth
add9	-	Major added Ninth
sus4	-	Suspended Fourth
7sus4	-	Dominant Seventh (susnded Fourth)
6/9	-	Six add Nine
dim	-	Diminished
sus	-	Suspended
aug	-	Augmented
7#9	-	Dominant Seventh

Printed in Great Britain
by Amazon